I0643921

TO

____

FROM

____

DATE

____

DAILY PRAYERS FOR MEN

DaySpring

Daily Prayers for Men
Copyright © 2024 DaySpring. All rights reserved.
First Edition, January 2024

Published by:

DaySpring

All rights reserved. No portion of this book may be reproduced, stored in a retrieval system, or transmitted in any form or by any means—electronic, mechanical, photocopy, recording, scanning, or other—except for brief quotations in critical reviews or articles, without the prior written permission of the publisher.

Published by Dayspring Books, an imprint of HarperCollins Christian Publishing, Inc. 501 Nelson Place, Nashville, TN 37214, USA.

Scripture quotations marked NLT are taken from the Holy Bible, New Living Translation, copyright © 1996, 2004, 2015 by Tyndale House Foundation. Used by permission of Tyndale House Publishers, Inc., Carol Stream, Illinois 60188. All rights reserved.

Scripture quotations marked ESV are taken from the ESV Bible® (The Holy Bible, English Standard Version®) copyright ©2001 by Crossway Bibles, a publishing ministry of Good News Publishers. Used by permission. All rights reserved.

Scripture quotations marked CSB® are taken from the Christian Standard Bible®, Copyright © 2017 by Holman Bible Publishers. Used by permission. Christian Standard Bible®, and CSB® are federally registered trademarks of Holman Bible Publishers.

Scripture quotations marked GNT are taken from the Good News Translation in Today's English Version- Second Edition Copyright © 1992 by American Bible Society. Used by Permission.

Scripture quotations marked NIV are taken from the Holy Bible, New International Version®, NIV®. Copyright © 1973, 1978, 1984, 2011 by Biblica, Inc.® Used by permission of Zondervan. All rights reserved worldwide. www.zondervan.com. The "NIV" and "New International Version" are trademarks registered in the United States Patent and Trademark Office by Biblica, Inc.®

Scripture quotations marked NASB are taken from the NEW AMERICAN STANDARD BIBLE ®, © Copyright 1960, 1962, 1963, 1968, 1971, 1972, 1973, 1975, 1977, 1995 by the Lockman Foundation. Used by permission. (www.lockman.org)

Scripture quotations marked NKJV are taken from the New King James Version. Copyright © 1982 by Thomas Nelson, Inc. Used by permission. All rights reserved.

Written with the assistance of: Peachtree Publishing Services
Cover Design by: Gayle Raymer

DaySpring titles may be purchased in bulk for educational, business, fundraising, or sales promotional use. For information, please email SpecialMarkets@ThomasNelson.com.

Any internet addresses, phone numbers, or company or product information printed in this book are offered as a resource and are not intended in any way to be or to imply an endorsement by DaySpring, nor does DaySpring vouch for the existence, content, or services of these sites, phone numbers, companies, or products beyond the life of this book.

Without limiting the exclusive rights of any author, contributor or the publisher of this publication, any unauthorized use of this publication to train generative artificial intelligence (AI) technologies is expressly prohibited. HarperCollins also exercise their rights under Article 4(3) of the Digital Single Market Directive 2019/790 and expressly reserve this publication from the text and data mining exception.

HarperCollins Publishers, Macken House, 39/40 Mayor Street Upper, Dublin 1, D01 C9W8, Ireland (https://www.harpercollins.com)

ISBN: 978-1-64870-934-0

Printed in China
26 27 28 29 30 CPP 6 5 4 3 2

CONTENTS

Introduction 8
Pray Boldly 10
Stand Firm 12
Character Matters 14
Not Guilty 16
Equip Yourself 18
Reconcile First 20
Growing in Faith. 22
Stay Humble 24
Get Angry, but Don't Sin 26
Do for Others 28
Stay Sharp. 30
Know What You Believe and Why 32
Pursue Peace 34
Don't Believe Everything You Hear 36
Unload Your Anxiety. 38
Nurture a Thankful Attitude 40
Imitate Christ 42
Praise God. 44
Focus Your Thoughts 46
Be Optimistic 48
Turn the Other Cheek. 50
Pass It On 52
Sacrificial Love. 54
Speak the Truth in Love 56
Be Diligent. 58
Surround Yourself with Good People 60
Face Temptation with Confidence. 62
Choose the Right Path 64

Handle the Word of Truth 66
Give It All to God 68
Tame Your Tongue 70
Set Your Mind on Things Above 72
Strive for Unity 74
Count the Cost 76
Pray in Private 78
Taking Tomorrow for Granted 80
Know Your Strength 82
Saved by Grace 84
Put on the Armor of God 86
Stay Courageous 88
A Community of Faith 90
Walk by Faith 92
Learn to Worship 94
Be an Encourager 96
Build a Strong Foundation 98
Practice Patience 100
Forever Hope 102
Bear Fruit 104
God Is Patient 106
Celebrate Forgiveness 108
Everyone Welcome 110
Trust That Evil Will Be Punished 112
Let Your Light Shine 114
Speak Up 116
Memorize God's Word 118
Celebrate Tribulation? 120
"Who Do You Say I Am?" 122
Recruit Wise Counselors 124
Glorify God 126

Love One Another 128
A New You 130
Use Your Time Wisely 132
A Little Help with Your Prayers 134
A Friend Indeed 136
Keep Your Guard Up 138
Renew Your Strength 140
Embrace Real Love 142
Jesus Can Empathize 144
Practice Spiritual Self-Care 146
Find Real Contentment 148
Plant Wisely 150
The Pursuit of Wealth 152
When You Are Weak, God Is Strong 154
Endure Trials 156
Let the Bible Do Its Work 158
Rest for the Weary 160
Celebrate Creativity 162
God Will Supply Your Needs 164
Give Cheerfully 166
Embrace Humility 168
Honor Your Marriage 170
Be Transformed, Not Conformed 172
Stay Near to God 174
Defuse Arguments 176
Use Your God-Given Gift 178
Faithfully Endure 180
Take Responsibility 182
Start with Yourself 184
Set Your Priorities 186
Resist the Devil 188

INTRODUCTION

Don't worry about anything; instead, pray about everything. Tell God what you need, and thank Him for all He has done. Then you will experience God's peace, which exceeds anything we can understand. His peace will guard your hearts and minds as you live in Christ Jesus.

PHILIPPIANS 4:6–7 NLT

The offer is so amazing, you almost expect to see legal fine print under it. But there are no conditions or restrictions. This is an actual invitation from the Creator of the universe—to you.

Talk to Me—anytime, about anything. Tell Me what you need. Give Me your worries. Let me show You what genuine peace of mind feels like. Knowing how to accept the invitation and what to say to God can be a challenge, especially if you have little personal history with Him. This devotional meets that challenge head-on. Using a meditation on God's Word to set the tone, each devotion includes a complete prayer you can use to start a conversation with God. You are never alone. You can give everything to God—your pain, anxiety, doubts, fears, and struggles. Open a dialogue with Him and let it change your life. Find the peace that only prayer can bring.

PRAY BOLDLY

So let us come boldly to the throne of our gracious God. There we will receive His mercy, and we will find grace to help us when we need it most.

HEBREWS 4:16 NLT

To maximize the impact of your prayers, start with your approach. Take a moment to consider where you are and what a privilege it is to be there. Prayer transports you to the throne room of heaven for a personal encounter with the Creator and Sustainer of all. And you don't even need an appointment. You can boldly approach Him, knowing that He will never turn you away. Not because you've earned the honor, but because He is gracious. Jesus's sacrifice makes it possible for you to enter God's presence. You can take any request to Him, not because *you* know what needs to be done, but because you know *He* does. Jesus taught His disciples to pray, "May Your will be done" (Matthew 6:10 NLT). That's the target to aim for when you pray—that God's will, not yours, be done. God's will being done guarantees the best possible outcome. When you link your will with His, you can boldly enter His presence any time, knowing that your prayer will be answered.

God, thank You for the privilege of entering Your presence. The fact that I'm able to talk to You one-on-one is so overwhelming that it doesn't always fully register. I am humbled by the opportunity to talk and listen to You. Guide my thoughts and desires as I pray so that they align with Your will.

LET ME NEVER LOSE SIGHT OF YOUR MERCY AND GRACE IN MY LIFE.

AMEN.

STAND FIRM

Be watchful, stand firm in the faith, act like men, be strong.

I CORINTHIANS 16:13 ESV

When someone tells you to "act like a man," what message do you hear? Be tough? Hide your feelings? Take down a bully? Don't show vulnerability? Suffer in silence? This verse offers some helpful hints on what those words mean when they come from God. "Stand firm in the faith" encourages you to examine your foundation. Understand why you believe what you do. Don't be afraid to ask tough questions. Get to know God's Word. Reinforce your own faith so that you can help others stand firm with you. Notice that God says, "Be strong," not, "Maintain a strong facade." This verse isn't talking about hiding your vulnerabilities or pretending you don't have any. Sometimes the strongest thing you can do is admit your weakness and ask for help. With the help of God and the people who care about you, you can stand strong through any circumstances.

God, thank You for Your perspective on what it means to act like a man. Thank You for freeing me from having to put up a facade or conform to certain cultural expectations about how a man should act. Help me understand what it means to stand firm in my faith. Give me the right questions to ask as I try to figure out why I believe what I do. Surround me with people who can help me examine and strengthen my foundation. I want to be strong–for myself and for others. Show me how. Give me the courage to admit my weaknesses and ask for help when I need it. Hold my feet steady so that I won't back down from challenges to my faith.

HELP ME BECOME THE MAN
YOU CREATED ME TO BE.
AMEN.

CHARACTER MATTERS

A good name is to be chosen over great wealth; favor is better than silver and gold.

PROVERBS 22:1 CSB

How many times have you heard a kid say, "When I grow up, I want to have a reputation for integrity"? Our culture often celebrates wealth and power over good character (though wealth and power can be used to accomplish good things). Solomon, a wise king who wrote much of the book of Proverbs, suggests a different priority. It's a suggestion worth considering, seeing as how Solomon enjoyed more power and wealth than perhaps anyone else in history. Solomon's advice is to pursue integrity, to build a good name for yourself in everything you do. You do that by giving your all in your every endeavor. By striving for quality and being fair in your dealings. By giving others the benefit of the doubt and showing love to your enemies. By going the extra mile for people who insult you. You do it by noticing people who rarely get noticed. By demonstrating through your words and actions that they matter. You do it by following Jesus's example.

God, thank You for the timeless advice in Your Word. Thank You for the example of Solomon, who spoke from experience. He had the power and wealth that most people dream of, but he learned what was truly important in life and chose to share what he learned with others. Thank You for working through him to teach us the importance of integrity. Guide me as I work to create a good name for myself, a name that reflects Your character and Your love. Show me the path of integrity in everything I do.

AND I WILL GIVE YOU
ALL THE GLORY.
AMEN.

NOT GUILTY

But if we confess our sins to God,
He will keep His promise and do what is right:
He will forgive us our sins and purify us from all wrongdoing.

I JOHN 1:9 GNT

For many people, guilt is one of the heaviest emotional burdens to carry. But it doesn't have to be. That's not what God intends. In God's plan, guilt serves an important purpose, like a flashing light on your car's dashboard. Or a physical symptom that makes you concerned about your health. Or a malware alert from your computer. Or a tornado siren in your area. Guilt is a warning. It lets you know that you've done something to damage your relationship with God or with another person—or with both. Guilt brings the problem to your attention and gives you the opportunity to do something about it. Guilt isn't a ball and chain that you have to wear for the rest of your life. It's a reminder to take your emotional burden to the One who can relieve it. If you confess your wrongdoing to God, He will forgive you. He will also take away your guilt, if you'll let Him. You can stand before Him and others guilt-free.

God, thank You for not making me carry my guilt. At the same time, however, thank You for using guilt to let me know when I've damaged my relationship with You or with others. Thank You for caring that much about my relationships. Show me what the best response to guilt looks like. Give me the wisdom to make amends to people I've hurt and repair broken relationships. Remind me to turn to You and acknowledge when I have hurt You or other people.

HELP ME TO ASK FOR, EXPERIENCE, AND ENJOY YOUR FORGIVENESS.

AMEN.

EQUIP YOURSELF

All Scripture is God-breathed and is useful for teaching, rebuking, correcting and training in righteousness, so that the servant of God may be thoroughly equipped for every good work.

II TIMOTHY 3:16-17 NIV

No experienced camper would set out for a weeklong adventure at a remote site without ensuring he's thoroughly equipped for the excursion. Things can go really wrong, really quickly, without the right preparation. The same goes for practically any other adventure, including skiing, fishing, rock climbing, and rafting. Similarly, God gave you His Word to equip you for the path He's laid out for you. Everything you need to know about Him and His plan for your life is found in it. The Bible teaches you His truth. It calls you out when you fall short. It corrects you when your priorities get scrambled. It trains you to resist temptation and keep your eyes on the goal. God's Word helps you fully appreciate the high points of your journey and endure the lows. It gives you the footing to take bold leaps of faith and the support to help you regain your balance when you stumble. Are you ready for your adventure?

Father, thank You for the adventure You've laid out before me. Thank You for Your Word, which prepares me for it and shows me how to avoid danger and distractions. Open my eyes to Your truth when I read it. Show me how I can apply it to my journey. Teach me Your ways. Call me out when I go astray. Correct me when I'm wrong. Train me to live in a righteous way. Equip me to carry out Your work.

HELP ME FULLY APPRECIATE EVERY LEG OF MY JOURNEY.

AMEN.

RECONCILE FIRST

"Therefore, if you are presenting your offering at the altar, and there you remember that your brother has something against you, leave your offering there before the altar and go; first be reconciled to your brother, and then come and present your offering."

MATTHEW 5:23–24 NASB

In Jesus's day, presenting an offering at the altar was a form of worshiping God—a way of honoring God by praising Him and focusing attention on Him. Worship draws you closer to God, but Jesus said that conflict with another person interrupts your relationship with God. And you need to fix it. Notice where the responsibility lies. If someone has something against you, *your* job is to take the first step toward reconciliation. It doesn't matter who's to blame. It doesn't matter what circumstances led to the conflict. Think of it as part of your offering to God. You sacrifice your pride and ego to make amends so that you can worship God with a clean relational slate. Romans 12:18 says, "If possible, so far as it depends on you, be at peace with all people" (NASB). If you work toward that goal, God will use your efforts to accomplish extraordinary things.

God, thank You for caring about my broken relationships. Thank You for placing such a priority on healing them. I don't want them to interfere with my relationship with You. Make me aware of the people I need to reconcile with. Remind me of the circumstances that led to each break. Give me the strength and humility I need to restore those relationships–or at least do my part in asking for forgiveness and working toward peace.

HELP ME PREPARE MY HEART SO THAT IT'S READY TO WORSHIP AND GLORIFY YOU.

AMEN.

GROWING IN FAITH

Be kindly affectionate to one another with brotherly love, in honor giving preference to one another; not lagging in diligence, fervent in spirit, serving the Lord; rejoicing in hope, patient in tribulation, continuing steadfastly in prayer; distributing to the needs of the saints, given to hospitality.

ROMANS 12:10–13 NKJV

This passage provides followers of Jesus with a snapshot of faith in action. It begins with love—finding ways to show genuine concern and affection for other people. Living and growing in faith in Jesus shows itself in a selfless spirit—allowing others to set an agenda instead of insisting on doing things your way. When you let go of your own agenda, you see what God can accomplish with His. As you grow in your faith, you'll learn to find joy where others see only despair. You'll learn to deal with trials and suffering with a patience you didn't think possible. You'll carve time out of your busy schedule for prayer because you've seen its power. You'll place a high priority on assisting spiritual "front-line workers" because you recognize the importance of their work. When you commit to growing in faith, yours is not the only life that will be changed.

God, thank You for giving me so much room to grow in my faith. Thank You for showing me in Your Word what faith has the potential to do. Guide me as I work to reach that potential. I understand that it won't be easy. But the rewards will far outweigh the effort. Show me what my next step is in growing my faith, and then the step after that. Bring people into my life who can help me. Help me to genuinely love others.

AND SHOW ME HOW TO MAKE A DIFFERENCE IN THE WORLD AROUND ME.

AMEN.

STAY HUMBLE

"For those who exalt themselves will be humbled, and those who humble themselves will be exalted."

LUKE 14:11 NLT

Jesus set the example for humble living, even though He was God in human form. He had every reason to exalt Himself. Instead, He set aside His heavenly privileges to come to earth as one of us—because that was the only way we could be saved. He chose to serve others. He washed His disciples' feet. He allowed Himself to be crucified. And throughout His life, He directed praise and glory to His heavenly Father. Jesus understood something essential about His Father—something He wants His followers to understand as well. When God gets 100 percent of the glory and honor—100 percent of the credit—amazing things happen. Broken lives are healed. Broken relationships are mended. Hope finds its way into hopeless situations. Only God can do the work necessary, so only He should get the praise. Your job is to do His will, to point the way to Him, and to lead the applause for Him when He delivers. That's what it means to be humble.

God, thank You for Your work in my life.

I know that everything good in it is from You.

Give me the perspective to see just how much good there is. I want to fully appreciate all that You do so that I'm not tempted to take credit for it.

Thank You for the constant reminders in Your Word to praise and glorify You.

Help me find new and creative ways to do that.

Let me never lose my sense of humility.

MAKE ME USEFUL TO YOU—
THAT'S ALL I ASK.
AMEN.

GET ANGRY, BUT DON'T SIN

Be angry and do not sin;
do not let the sun go down on your anger.

EPHESIANS 4:26 ESV

Anger is a valid emotion for God's people. The pain an injustice we experience in life often makes us angry. Notice that the verse from Ephesians treats anger as a given. It says of course you're angry. Now master your anger so that it doesn't master you. Don't give it a foothold in your life. Don't nurture a grudge. That's what happens when you let the sun go down on your anger. Anger festers, grows, and starts to invade other areas of your life. Have you ever blown up at a loved one because of your anger toward someone else? That's what happens when you leave anger unresolved. God's plan is for you to acknowledge your anger and take the necessary steps to deal with it. Pray about it. Ask God to help you understand the root of it. Confront the person or the issue that made you angry. Look for ways to reconcile. Let your anger serve its purpose and then let it go. You don't have to do it alone. God will give you everything you need to restore peace in your life.

God, thank You for understanding my emotions. Thank You for giving me a way to respond to the injustice, pain, and unfairness I encounter. Help me manage my anger so that it doesn't manage me. Give me the wisdom to recognize the best way to deal with my anger in a given situation. Give me the awareness to consider the impact of my anger on others.

GIVE ME THE SELF-CONTROL TO RELEASE MY ANGER AFTER IT HAS SERVED ITS PURPOSE.

AMEN.

DO FOR OTHERS

*Carry one another's burdens;
in this way you will fulfill the law of Christ.*

GALATIANS 6:2 CSB

This isn't a command to do someone else's heavy lifting. It's an invitation to share in the Lord's work. Jesus said, "Come to Me, all of you who are weary and burdened, and I will give you rest" (Matthew 11:28 CSB). And we can participate in Jesus's rest-giving ministry. The first step is to become aware of other people's burdens—to find out what people really need. We can do that by initiating relationships and making ourselves available to others, physically and emotionally. We can learn to ask the right questions and show people we truly care about what they are going through. Once we become aware of their burdens, we can help carry them. To do that, we need strength—not necessarily physical strength, but emotional and spiritual strength. The kind of strength that comes only through prayer and Bible study. Ask God to help you make a difference in other people's lives, and you'll be amazed at what you can do. And then make sure that He gets the credit.

God, thank You for carrying my burdens and giving me rest. Thank You for people in my life who have carried my burdens by listening to me, loving me, and supporting me. Thank You for giving me a chance to share in Jesus's work by carrying other people's burdens. Create in me a heart that is attuned to other people's needs. Give me the wisdom to ask the right questions. Give me the strength to carry other people's burdens.

REMIND ME TO GIVE YOU ALL THE CREDIT FOR IT.

AMEN.

STAY SHARP

Iron sharpens iron, and one person sharpens another.

PROVERBS 27:17 CSB

Iron can be sharpened only by something as solid and unyielding as it is. And when iron meets iron in the sharpening process, sparks fly. Solomon, the writer of most of the book of Proverbs, used the process as an ingenious analogy for the impact certain people have on us. "Iron sharpeners" are valuable friends to have in your corner. Iron sharpeners are solid. They've been molded by experience. They have personal, emotional, relational, and spiritual integrity. They don't change who they are to fit their circumstances. They're reliable. You can count on them to speak the truth, even when you may not want to hear it. Iron sharpeners will hold you accountable if you let them. They see where you are now and where you want to be, and they help track your progress. They will lovingly confront you when necessary and celebrate with you when appropriate. Iron sharpeners are gifts from God. They refine your rough edges and sharpen you. The process may not always be pretty or comfortable, but the results are striking.

God, thank You for the iron sharpeners in my life. My interactions with them may not always be pleasant, but they are important. Never let me lose sight of that. Give me the wisdom to consider their input and make necessary changes to my life. Help me know when to yield and when to push back. Help me recognize the sparks that fly as a necessary part of the process. Help me keep an open mind and a constant desire to grow and grind away my rough edges. Give me the opportunity to help others in return.

GIVE ME THE STRENGTH TO BE AN EFFECTIVE IRON SHARPENER. AMEN.

KNOW WHAT YOU BELIEVE AND WHY

But in your hearts revere Christ as Lord.
Always be prepared to give an answer to everyone
who asks you to give the reason for the hope that you have.
But do this with gentleness and respect.

1 PETER 3:15 NIV

We place our faith in countless things every day without a second thought. We place our faith in chairs to support us. In airplanes to stay aloft. In GPS systems to get us where we're going. If someone asked us to explain why, we could offer some compelling reasons. We may not understand the physics involved, but we've seen them work. This verse in First Peter makes it clear that we can do the same with the Christian faith. We can't see God, but we can see His handiwork in the natural world around us. We can't verify the supernatural origins of the Bible, but we can experience its power when we read it and incorporate its truths into our lives. We can't offer empirical evidence of the difference Jesus makes in our lives, but we can share our personal experiences. And that's often enough.

God, thank You for the hope You offer through Jesus. Thank You for giving me something substantial to put my faith in. Thank You that I can be confident that I will have eternal life after I die because of faith in Jesus. Help me see the big picture of Your plan–for my life and for the world. Guide me as I become acquainted with Your Word. Help me understand not just the "whats" but the "whys" too. Help me get to the point where I feel comfortable talking about what I believe and why. Equip me to answer the questions people ask.

HELP ME BE "ALWAYS PREPARED." AMEN.

PURSUE PEACE

Pursue peace with all people,
and the holiness without which no one will see the Lord.
See to it that no one comes short of the grace of God;
that no root of bitterness springing up causes trouble,
and by it many become defiled.

HEBREWS 12:14–15 NASB

These verses provide a blueprint for changing the world one community at a time. The first word reveals the radical nature of God's peace plan. *Pursue* is an action verb; in this case, it's phrased as a command. God won't settle for a passive, live-and-let-live approach to peace. He wants His people to *pursue peace. With all people.* Some people wage war. God wants us to wage peace. His Word encourages us to think hard about the way we interact with others. To walk away from foolish and unnecessary quarrels. To look for common ground instead of battlegrounds. To pray for patience and understanding. To turn the other cheek when people attack. That's how peace starts in God's plan. And that's how the world is changed.

God, thank You for prioritizing peace. Thank You for Your grassroots plan to achieve it. Give me a heart for peace as well. Show me things I can change in myself to help promote peace. If that means swallowing my pride or apologizing for things I've done, I ask You to help me do those things. Give me the courage to walk away from foolish quarrels. Help me find common ground with others. Give me the discipline to turn the other cheek. Show me how to pursue peace with my family, friends, coworkers, neighbors, and acquaintances–especially in those relationships where peace doesn't exist now.

LET THERE BE PEACE ON EARTH,

AND LET IT BEGIN WITH ME.

AMEN.

DON'T BELIEVE EVERYTHING YOU HEAR

Beloved, do not believe every spirit,
but test the spirits, whether they are of God;
because many false prophets have gone out into the world.

I JOHN 4:1 NKJV

False teachers were the scammers of Jesus's day. They pretended to be people they were not. They spoke messages that sounded like the truth. And they preyed on vulnerable people—in this case, new Christians who knew little about their faith. God offered a simple solution to the problem of false teachers—one that still works today: put their messages to the test. Judge them against the truth of God's Word. The Bible is the standard of truth. Anyone who contradicts it or changes its message is a false teacher. If you don't know the Bible well enough yet to make those comparisons, look for a trusted Christian friend or mentor to help you.

God, thank You for giving me a starting point in my search for spiritual truth. It's an amazing thing to know I can trust every promise in Your Word. Help me understand why the truth of the Bible must be protected at all costs. Guide me as I try to learn those truths. Show me how to apply them in my daily walk. Bring spiritual mentors into my life who can help build my Christian faith. Show me how to test the teachings I hear at church, in the media, or in my daily life against the truth of Your Word. Give me the right questions to ask. Help me recognize patterns to look for. When I pray and listen silently for Your response, make me aware of my own misunderstandings of Your Word.

HELP ME BUILD A SPIRITUAL FOUNDATION ON SOLID TRUTH.

AMEN.

UNLOAD YOUR ANXIETY

***Give all your worries and cares to God,
for He cares about you.***

I PETER 5:7 NLT

The Bible is full of amazing truths, but none more so than the last four words in this verse. *He cares about you*. The God of the Bible, the Creator and Sustainer of the universe, cares about you. No matter what you've done in the past, no matter how other people feel about you, no matter how you feel about Him—or how you feel about yourself—God cares for you. Not in some abstract way. He cares about every emotional struggle, every bout with anxiety, every moment you feel overwhelmed. And He issues an invitation for every one of them: *Give it to Me. Don't try to lift this one yourself. Don't try to endure the unendurable. Let Me help you*. You never have to go it alone.

God, it's amazing to realize that the One who created the heavens and the earth, whose power is greater than any other, who can see all of eternity, cares about the smallest details of my life. Thank You for Your loving concern. You know the guilt I carry. You know the habits I struggle to break. You know the conflicts I'm involved in. You know my high highs and my low lows. You know the self-image issues I struggle with. You see the holes in my heart and know what caused them. You know my doubts and fears. You know my concerns about the future. You know the questions I need answered. You know everything about me and still care. Help me see the wisdom in giving You my worries and cares. Show me how to do that. I know I can't carry them alone.

I NEED YOU.

AMEN.

NURTURE A THANKFUL ATTITUDE

Give thanks in all circumstances;
for this is the will of God in Christ Jesus for you.

I THESSALONIANS 5:18 ESV

Choose your approach to life. That's the message of this verse. From one perspective, the world is full of annoyances. You can find something to be perturbed about at least once an hour if that's what you're looking for. From another perspective, the world is full of danger. You can find something to be worried about around every corner if you let your fears dictate. From yet another perspective, the world is full of God's blessings. You can find evidence of His amazing work not just in every corner of the universe but also in every corner of your life. The question is, which perspective will you choose? Because it really is a matter of choice. If you choose to view the world through the lens of God's blessings, you'll be able to give thanks in all circumstances. You'll see that good results can come from bad circumstances. You'll see that challenges sharpen us and make us stronger. And you'll see that God's goodness often hides in plain sight all around us.

God, thank You. I may not always recognize Your blessings in my life or Your work in the world around me, but I want to. Show me just how much I have to be thankful for. Help me see the wisdom in choosing to see the world as being full of Your blessings. Let me experience the joy that comes from choosing that approach to life. Show me how to give thanks in circumstances that don't normally inspire thankfulness. Teach me how to maintain a spirit of thanksgiving all year round.

AMEN.

IMITATE CHRIST

Imitate me, then, just as I imitate Christ. I praise you because you always remember me and follow the teachings that I have handed on to you.

I CORINTHIANS 11:1–2 GNT

On one end of the spectrum, you have the demand of certain authority figures: "Do as I say, not as I do." At the other end of the spectrum, you have these verse from I Corinthians. Paul, the church leader who wrote these words, set the bar high for Christian mentors. It takes quite a commitment to say, "Watch me and follow my example because I'm doing my best to live like Jesus did." Yet that's exactly what new believers and people who are curious about Christianity need. It's one thing to hear someone teach about what it means to be a follower of Jesus. It's quite another thing to see how a Christian acts in real-life situations. Or how he interacts with other Christians. Or how he reacts when he's happy, disappointed, angry, or sad. If you want to understand Jesus, look for a mentor who is imitating Him.

God, thank You for Jesus, who set the example for the way we should live. He didn't just say, "Do as I say"; He modeled everything He wants us to do. Thank You for recording Jesus's life in Your Word so that we don't have to wonder about what He did. Help me get comfortable with studying Your Word. Thank You for the people in my life who can help me in that area. Help me connect with others who are serious about following Jesus–people who try to imitate Him in the things they say and do.

GIVE ME THE PERSPECTIVE TO SEE WHAT JESUS IS LIKE THROUGH THEM.

AMEN.

PRAISE GOD

I will praise God's name with song and exalt Him with thanksgiving.

PSALM 69:30 CSB

European football is a mystery to many American sports fans. They wonder how 90,000 people can cheer wildly for 90-plus minutes for a contest that might end in a 0–0 draw. The answer, of course, is in the nuances of the game. The more you understand about what's happening on the pitch, the easier it is to cheer. The same is true with praising God—that is, telling Him how great He is. That's something God wants from His people—something we can do to please Him. For someone new to the Christian faith, to "praise God's name with song and exalt Him with thanksgiving" could be confusing. After all, how many times can you praise God for being, say, good or powerful? The answer is beyond calculation—if you look for the nuances of His goodness and power. That's how we keep our praise fresh: by constantly looking for new examples of His goodness, power, and other attributes in our lives. No one has ever regretted finding new and meaningful ways to praise God.

God, You are amazing. I don't know how many ways I can say that, but I want to find out. I want to learn to praise You in ways that are personal. I want to create a unique relationship with You. Open my eyes to the countless things around me that I can praise You for–from the beauty of the natural world to the people who care about me. Let me see Your fingerprints all over the good things in this world and in my life.

HELP ME LEARN TO
APPRECIATE YOU MORE.
AMEN.

FOCUS YOUR THOUGHTS

In conclusion, my friends, fill your minds with those things that are good and that deserve praise: things that are true, noble, right, pure, lovely, and honorable.

PHILIPPIANS 4:8 GNT

At any given moment, how many things are jockeying for position in your mind? How many ideas, thoughts, plans, memories, and images are trying to take center stage—trying to get you to focus on them? How do you decide the "winner" at any given moment? All too often, we allow our mood to dictate what we think about. If we're feeling angry, we might dwell on past offenses. If we're feeling lonely, we might imagine other people having fun together without us. If we're not careful, we can get caught in a loop of angry thoughts leading to more anger or lonely thoughts leading to deeper loneliness. God's Word recommends installing a gatekeeper for our thoughts—a sort of "gray matter bouncer" that examines individual thoughts before either allowing or denying them entrance. The right thoughts, after all, can bring us closer to God, give us clarity, and improve our well-being.

Father, thank You for the amazing potential of my mind. Thank You for the ability to choose the things I dwell on. Remind me that I have that choice when certain types of thoughts try to dominate. Thank You for surrounding me with so many good things to think about. Help me focus my thoughts on those good things when my mind starts to wander. Show me how to bolster my mental health, strengthen my faith, and grow closer to You by filling my mind with things that are true, noble, right, pure, lovely, and honorable.

AMEN.

BE OPTIMISTIC

"For I know the plans I have for you," declares the LORD, "plans to prosper you and not to harm you, plans to give you hope and a future."

JEREMIAH 29:11 NIV

This verse piques curiosity. Talk of "plans to prosper you and . . . give you hope" makes us eager to know what the finished project will look like. Who wouldn't like at least a glimpse of the prosperous and hope-filled future that awaits us? But the "present us" isn't prepared to see the "future us." God promises to prosper us and give us hope, but that doesn't mean there won't be setbacks, heartbreaks, tragedies, and challenges along the way. If God were to reveal them now, we might lose our optimism about the future and start to question our ability to handle what's to come. Thankfully, God's plans for the future include Him walking with us every step of the way, equipping us to deal with each challenge and setback as it comes, helping us grow and mature, and giving us hard-earned wisdom and resilience. That's why we can have hope, no matter what the future holds.

God, thank You for giving me so much to look forward to. As the saying goes, "I don't know what the future holds, but I know who holds the future." And though I may be curious, I really don't need to know any more than that.

You can see what's to come in my life as clearly as you can see what's already happened.

So I trust You to prepare me for it.

If I start to feel anxious or pessimistic about what the future holds, remind me that You have plans to give me hope and a future.

AMEN.

TURN THE OTHER CHEEK

"You have heard that it was said,
'An eye for an eye and a tooth for a tooth.'
But I tell you not to resist an evil person.
But whoever slaps you on your right cheek,
turn the other to him also."

MATTHEW 5:38–39 NKJV

"An eye for an eye," the law of retaliation, is a popular approach to justice. If someone harms you, you get to harm them in an equal way to settle the score. The problem, of course, is that the retaliation is rarely equal. So instead of justice, you get escalation. And, as someone once pointed out, "An eye for an eye leaves the whole world blind." Jesus understood that only a radical approach to justice can bring about peace. And turning the other cheek to someone who's just slapped you is pretty radical. When you absorb someone's effort to harm you without retaliating, you immediately de-escalate the situation. Even better, you take justice out of your own hands. You no longer have to keep a mental ledger of who's owed what. You can leave it in God's hands and trust Him to bring about true justice.

God, thank You for the wisdom of Your Son. Thank You for the example He set in living out this principle. When people lied about Him, He stayed silent. When people hit Him, He refused to retaliate. He left justice to You. Give me the courage to follow His example when people harm me. Give me the strength to resist the urge to retaliate. Give me the discipline to take the high road by turning the other cheek and avoiding escalating the situation. Remind me that Your justice is perfect.

LET PEACE BEGIN WITH ME.

AMEN.

PASS IT ON

If you help the poor, you are lending to the LORD—and He will repay you!

PROVERBS 19:17 NLT

With apologies to *The Lion King,* this verse reveals the true "circle of life." God generously gives blessings to people—skills, talents, finances, material possessions. Those people, in turn, generously share their blessings with the poor. The poor, in turn, give thanks to God for His goodness. Everyone plays a role. The poor are taken care of, God is praised, and God's people get to share in His work. The Bible doesn't often give people the chance to do something for God, so this is a rare opportunity. God opens your eyes to the needs of others for a reason. His heart is with the poor, the people who fall through the cracks. If your heart is with them, too, you'll find that your shared interest brings you closer to Him. God gives us the power to change the world around us—and to lend to Him in the process. We would be wise to take full advantage of the opportunity. The interest He pays is life-changing.

God, thank You for caring about the people who slip through the cracks in our world. Thank You for giving me a chance to help others. I will not take the opportunity lightly. Open my eyes to the struggles of the people around me. Show me specific ways that I can make a difference. Let me never be the end point of Your blessings but rather a middleman who passes them on to others. Give me an appreciation for the things I've been given— not just material possessions, but my skills, energy, and time as well.

HELP ME FIND CREATIVE WAYS TO USE THEM TO HELP OTHERS. AMEN.

SACRIFICIAL LOVE

Husbands, love your wives, as Christ loved the church and gave himself up for her.

EPHESIANS 5:25 ESV

If everyone took marriage as seriously as God does, divorce lawyers would be in trouble. In the analogy this verse sets up, husbands are aligned with Jesus. Expectations don't get any higher than that. That doesn't mean God expects husbands to love their wives perfectly, as Jesus loves His people. What it does mean is that God takes marriage vows seriously—and He expects us to take them seriously too. Sacrifice is the key. If you're married, this means giving up your own wants and needs for the sake of your spouse. Prioritizing her. Setting aside time to spend with her. Learning the most effective ways to show her love. Discovering the words and actions that resonate deep within her. Even if you're not married, if you are a man who commits to loving the people in your life in a sacrificial, meaningful way, God will deepen your relationships in ways you can't imagine.

God, thank You for giving us the example of a committed marriage relationship to show us how to love the people You've placed in our lives. Thank You for wanting the absolute best for my relationships. And thank You for Jesus's example of what sacrificial love looks like. Teach me to hang on loosely to my own wants and needs so that I can forgo them as needed. Help me manage my time so that others receive from me more than whatever's left after work and my other responsibilities. Give me the wisdom to reset my priorities as often as necessary to assure the people I love of their importance. Help me anticipate their needs and communicate my love in ways that are especially meaningful.

AMEN.

SPEAK THE TRUTH IN LOVE

But speaking the truth in love,
let us grow in every way into Him who is the Head—Christ.

EPHESIANS 4:15 CSB

When you consider the most valuable people in your life, don't overlook the concerned truth tellers. These people find loving ways to inform you of things you may not want to hear—but need to hear. They take you aside when they see you fall back on old, dangerous behavior. They give you pep talks when they see you settle for less than your best. It takes courage to be that person. To risk rejection and anger. To have your motives questioned. It takes love to be that person effectively. To learn to say the right things at the right time in a way that communicates care and concern, instead of judgment. This verse challenges us to be that person in other people's lives. It's not hard to find people who will tell you what you want to hear. But the person who will tell you what you need to hear, in a way that builds up instead of tearing down, is a valuable ally indeed. That's what God wants all of His people to be.

God, thank You for the people in my life who have the courage and compassion to speak the truth to me in a loving way. Forgive me for the times I didn't respond as I should have. No matter how hard it is to hear the truth, I understand that You love me too much to let me stay unaware of it. Give me the courage to say difficult things to the people I love. Give me the wisdom and compassion to be able to say those necessary things in a loving way.

LET MY WORDS BE RECEIVED
AS THEY ARE INTENDED.
AMEN.

BE DILIGENT

How long is the lazy man going to lie around? When is he ever going to get up? "I'll just take a short nap," he says; "I'll fold my hands and rest a while." But while he sleeps, poverty will attack him like an armed robber.

PROVERBS 6:9–11 GNT

Practical advice is timeless. What was true 2,500 years ago is still true today. Laziness is a stealth destroyer; it does damage without our realizing it. Case in point: a nap is a harmless diversion. No one would begrudge someone a short rest, but badly timed diversions, no matter how harmless they seem, take our attention away from what we should be doing. The results come quickly and devastatingly. The message of this verse is to work in season and rest in season. Not just in your vocation, but in every area of your life, including your well-being and your relationships. God created us to find purpose and fulfillment in all kinds of work. Our capacity for work is one of the things we have in common with Him. God wants us to be diligent workers because He is a diligent worker. When we embrace work as He does, we grow closer to Him.

Father, thank You for the timeless wisdom and the wake-up calls in Your Word. Thank You for showing me how to accomplish more. Thank You for creating me to find purpose and fulfillment in work. Let me never lose sight of the connection between work and emotional well-being. Help me recognize and work toward an ideal balance of work and rest. Show me what laziness looks like in my own life so that I can avoid it. Give me the motivation to do my best in the work You have laid out for me.

AMEN.

SURROUND YOURSELF WITH GOOD PEOPLE

Do not be misled: "Bad company corrupts good character."

I CORINTHIANS 15:33 NIV

No matter how perceptive we think we are in assessing people's character, the reality is, we all have blind spots—areas in which our shrewdness fails. These blind spots may be caused by a misreading of people's intentions, a desire to see the good in everyone, or the enjoyment of someone's company. Whatever the cause, these blind spots cause us to lower our guard or underestimate the threat of negative influences. We reckon that our positive influence will sway others more than their negative influence will sway us. Unfortunately, that's not always the case, as this verse makes clear. These words from I Corinthians urge us to look objectively at the influence of other people in our lives. They remind us to set firm boundaries with people who negatively affect our attitudes and our reputation. Who threaten our hard-earned sobriety or healthy lifestyle. Who hinder our spiritual growth. "Bad company corrupts good character" is not a call to judge others; it's a reminder that relationships are a huge part of who we are.

God, thank You for the good people in my life.
The people who care about me and support me.
The people who want to see me grow.
The people who influence me in a positive way.
Thank You also for the opportunity to be a good influence in other people's lives. Help me be the friend, mentor, or listening ear they need.
At the same time, give me the wisdom to recognize bad company in my own life.
Give me the courage to set the necessary boundaries to guard my physical, mental, emotional, and spiritual health.

AMEN.

FACE TEMPTATION WITH CONFIDENCE

No temptation has overtaken you except something common to mankind; and God is faithful, so He will not allow you to be tempted beyond what you are able, but with the temptation will provide the way of escape also, so that you will be able to endure it.

I CORINTHIANS 10:13 NASB

Few things rattle a person's self-confidence like temptation. Just when you start to feel good about your discipline and self-control, a blast of temptation will weave its way past your defenses and strike where you're most vulnerable. This verse reveals a few truths about temptation that can lessen its impact. First, temptation works best when it isolates you and makes you think you're the only one facing it. But the truth is, everyone wrestles with temptation. Whatever's tempting you is tempting others. Second, God knows the limits of your resistance and won't let you be pushed beyond them. Third, there is a way out, no matter what you're facing. That's God promise. So you can have hope, no matter how many times you've given in to a temptation in the past. If you call on God when you're tempted, He will lead you out.

God, thank You for caring so much for me even when I struggle with temptation in my life. Thank You for knowing my limits and making sure that I don't get pushed past them. Thank You for Your promise that You will provide a way out of every temptation I face. Remind me to turn to You right away when I feel tempted. Show me the best escape route. Give me the strength to resist.

I WANT TO HONOR YOU WITH THE CHOICES I MAKE.

AMEN.

CHOOSE THE RIGHT PATH

Jesus said to him, "I am the way, the truth, and the life. No one comes to the Father except through Me."

JOHN 14:6 NKJV

In two sentences, Jesus reveals how He saves us from a lifetime of spiritual searching and confusion. Some well-meaning people claim that all paths lead to God—that it doesn't matter *what* you believe, as long as you believe something. But Jesus says that only one path leads to God, and that's Him. God created humankind with the ability to choose right or wrong. Choosing wrong separates us from Him because He's perfectly holy. He can have no connection with sin. He's also perfectly just. He must punish all sin. And the punishment for sin is death. Only a perfect sacrifice could satisfy God's holiness and justice and make eternal life possible. Someone without sin had to die in our place. That's why Jesus came to earth: to live a sinless life, die in our place, and break the power of death by rising from the grave. The words in this verse come from the ultimate authority. Jesus is the only way to eternal life with God.

God, thank You for loving me so much that You provided a way for me to connect with You. Thank You for sacrificing Your only Son to make that connection possible. Forgive me for the sin that separated me from You. I believe that Jesus is the only way to be saved from the punishment for my sin—and the only way to eternal life. Help me fully understand what Jesus's sacrifice means and why all paths do not lead to You. Give me the perspective to recognize falsehoods in other teachings so that I don't get confused.

GUIDE ME IN FOLLOWING THE WAY JESUS LEADS.

AMEN.

HANDLE THE WORD OF TRUTH

Work hard so you can present yourself to God and receive His approval. Be a good worker, one who does not need to be ashamed and who correctly explains the word of truth.

II TIMOTHY 2:15 NLT

Think of a skill you've mastered. Juggling? Learning a second language? You probably didn't master the skill right away. You may have even considered it hopeless at first. That's the reaction of many people who open the Bible for the first time. And the twentieth time. Many are intimidated by the size and density of God's Word and confused by the language and ancient customs. But like other skills you've mastered, the more time you put into it, the easier it becomes. However, the first two words of this verse are "Work hard." But what separates learning God's Word from other pursuits is that God rewards every attempt to understand the Bible. He sheds light on difficult passages. He opens your mind to new teachings. He helps you connect the dots between biblical principles and real-life application. If you're serious about learning God's Word, He's serious about tutoring you.

God, thank You for Your Word.
In a culture where "truth" is often hard to recognize, I know that everything in Your Word is true and dependable. Give me the perspective I need to approach Your Word with confidence. Help me find a study method that works for me. Bless the effort I put in to understanding it. Show me how to apply its truths to my daily life. And then please give me the wisdom and the understanding to clearly share those truths with the people

YOU'VE PLACED IN MY LIFE.

AMEN.

GIVE IT ALL TO GOD

Commit to the Lord whatever you do,
and He will establish your plans.

PROVERBS 16:3 NIV

Some people struggle with trust issues—and for good reason. They've placed their confidence in the wrong people in the past and been burned by it. Sometimes the emotional scars of those burns never go away. It's only natural that the more often you get let down by others, the less likely you are to trust again. Solomon, the wise king who wrote much of Proverbs, recommends a safer emotional investment strategy. Place your trust in God, who is always faithful and always dependable, and always rewards people's trust. Whatever you have in mind to do, take it to God in prayer first. Talk to Him about it. Share your excitement or anxiety with Him. Pose your questions. Express your doubts. Examine your motivation. Invite Him to guide your plans and direct you to the paths He would have you take. Not only will He guide you, but He will also accompany you, giving you the encouragement, motivation, and strength you need along the way.

God, thank You for caring so deeply about everything I do. Thank You for always being ready to listen to and talk with me. Thank You for rewarding my trust. Forgive me for times when I may seem reluctant to trust You. Help me overcome my past experiences with broken trust. Let me never lose sight of the wisdom of committing my plans to You. Help me understand that nothing in my life is too big for You to handle or too small for You to care about. Take control of my plans. Guide me down the paths you want me to take.

GIVE ME A SENSE OF PEACE ABOUT WHERE THEY WILL TAKE ME.

AMEN.

TAME YOUR TONGUE

The one who guards his mouth and tongue keeps himself out of trouble.

PROVERBS 21:23 CSB

The people who wrote the Bible were awed by the power of the tongue. The New Testament writer James marveled that one body part could do such good and such evil in equal measure. He compared the tongue to the rudder of a ship, a small device that can control an enormous vessel. More ominously, he compared it to a small blaze that can burn down an entire forest. Proverbs 21:23 clearly describes the danger the tongue presents—to the people who speak and to the people who hear. The safeguards that are recommended in this verse are like those you might apply to a weapon. Behind these safeguards, however, is an implicit promise. If we make a genuine effort to control our tongue, God will add His hand to the endeavor. He will remind us to think before we speak. He will show us ways to uplift instead of tear down. He will help us stay out of trouble.

God, thank You for giving me the tools I need to control my tongue. Help me learn to be a wise gatekeeper of my words. To think before I speak. To guard against saying things I will regret later. Proverbs 18:21 says, "Death and life are in the power of the tongue" (CSB)*. Help me use my words to make life better for the people around me. Help me build a reputation as someone who speaks the truth in a loving way. Someone who is quick to praise and slow to criticize. Someone who avoids gossip and other destructive uses of my tongue.*

GIVE ME THE STRENGTH AND DISCIPLINE TO MASTER MY WORDS. AMEN.

SET YOUR MIND ON THINGS ABOVE

You have been raised to life with Christ, so set your hearts on the things that are in heaven, where Christ sits on His throne at the right side of God. Keep your minds fixed on things there, not on things here on earth.

COLOSSIANS 3:1–2 GNT

If you are a follower of Jesus, you've been given a new headquarters, so to speak. Before you trusted in Jesus, you took your cues from the culture around you. Your beliefs were formed within the culture. Your priorities were established along cultural norms. Your behavior reflected your upbringing in the culture. Obviously, you filtered your beliefs, priorities, and behavior through your own unique personality, but their origins came from the culture. As a Christian, your headquarters is heaven. You take your cues from God. Instead of relying on the culture around you for inspiration, guidance, and hope, you can look to God's Word—to the promises He gives and the wisdom He offers. You can build your life on His solid foundation. You can trust in Him for eternal life.

God, thank You for shifting my focus upward and giving me something incredible to look forward to. No matter how unbearable life here on earth gets, I know it's only temporary. I know because You promise eternal life to everyone who believes in Jesus. And Your promises can always be trusted. When I feel anxious or overwhelmed, I can shift my focus and imagine what life will be like in a place where anxiety and emotional overload don't exist. Let me never lose sight of Your promise that something better is coming. Give me the wisdom to recognize what is truly important in the big picture of eternity so that I can focus on those things.

AMEN.

STRIVE FOR UNITY

***I appeal to you, brothers and sisters,
in the name of our Lord Jesus Christ,
that all of you agree with one another in what you say
and that there be no divisions among you,
but that you be perfectly united in mind and thought.***

I CORINTHIANS 1:10 NIV

The word *fellowship* refers to the unity that comes from Christians' shared beliefs, priorities, and behaviors. Ideally, that unity motivates us to cooperate with one another in worshiping God and doing His work. That's God's plan for His people. But fellowship is a tricky thing. Every church is made up of a diverse group of individuals, with a diverse set of personalities and preferences. Care must be taken to preserve fellowship. Today's verse encourages us to celebrate the things we have in common. Our common ground includes our love for Jesus, our thankfulness for His sacrifice, our interest in God's Word, and our mission to tell others about Jesus. Fellowship is an amazing gift from God. We must never underestimate its importance—in the church and in our lives.

God, thank You for the chance to experience real unity. Thank You for making it possible for a diverse group of believers to come together to worship and work side by side. Nurture in me a spirit that celebrates the diversity in my church. Help me understand and appreciate the things that unite me with my fellow believers. Give me the wisdom to recognize things that might interfere with our unity, such as pride or stubbornness. Create in me a humble spirit so that I will not get in the way of fellowship.

HELP ME BE "PERFECTLY UNITED IN MIND AND THOUGHT" WITH OTHERS IN MY CHURCH.

AMEN.

COUNT THE COST

"For what good does it do a person
if he gains the whole world,
but loses or forfeits himself?"

LUKE 9:25 NASB

What will this cost? Obviously, it's a great question to ask about any financial transaction. You don't want to commit to a purchase without knowing the exact amount you'll be required to pay. But it's also a great question to ask in other areas of life. Success in your career, for example. How much of your time, attention, and energy will it take? What will the cost be to your family? Your free time? Your emotional health? And, perhaps most important of all, how will it affect your relationship with Jesus? That must be your top priority. If your career demands first place in your life, the cost is too high. Likewise, if success means sacrificing biblical principles such as honesty, integrity, and sacrificial love, the cost is too high. Gaining even the whole world is not worth losing your identity in Jesus.

God, thank You for reminding me of what's truly important. Forgive me for times in the past when I didn't count the cost. Remind me that when I pursue a goal, whether it's achieving success in my career or making a relationship work, other areas of my life might suffer. Everything has a cost. Help me make Jesus's question in Luke 9 part of every goal I pursue. Deepen my appreciation for the truly valuable things in my life—my family and especially my relationship with Jesus—so that I can accurately assess their value. Give me the perspective to consider what I'm losing or forfeiting and to decide whether the gain is worth the cost.

HELP ME KEEP MY PRIORITIES STRAIGHT IN THE BUSYNESS OF DAILY LIFE.

AMEN.

PRAY IN PRIVATE

"And when you pray, you shall not be like the hypocrites. For they love to pray standing in the synagogues and on the corners of the streets, that they may be seen by men. Assuredly, I say to you, they have their reward. But you, when you pray, go into your room, and when you have shut your door, pray to your Father who is in the secret place; and your Father who sees in secret will reward you openly."

MATTHEW 6:5–6 NKJV

There were religious leaders in Jesus's day who turned their prayers into performances. They would stand in public places and draw attention to themselves by delivering elaborate, dramatic, and showy prayers. Jesus points out that these people didn't recognize the opportunity they were squandering. Prayer is an opportunity to speak with the Creator of the universe—who wants to have an intimate conversation with us. Prayer is a chance to strengthen our personal relationship with Him, to engage Him in every area of our lives. Prayer is about seeking His will and His grace, not about impressing others.

God, thank You for the privilege of speaking to You right now. Let me never take it for granted. I know that I've done nothing to earn the privilege. I know that I'm able to pray to You only because of Jesus's sacrifice. He bridged the gap between us. And I will make the most of my opportunity. Thank You for letting me speak to You from the heart, instead of requiring me to prepare perfectly worded prayers. Thank You for not making me impress You with my religious authority or speaking ability. Help me avoid the temptation of praying in a way that draws attention to me. All I want is to experience Your presence in an intimate conversation.

AMEN.

TAKING TOMORROW FOR GRANTED

Don't brag about tomorrow,
since you don't know what the day will bring.

PROVERBS 27:1 NLT

These are the words of perhaps the wisest man who ever lived. When Solomon became king of Israel, God promised to give him anything he wanted. Solomon asked for wisdom. In the book of Proverbs, he shares some of that wisdom: don't treat tomorrow as a given. It's a simple reminder, but one with enormous implications. His today-first approach to life can transform our relationships, among other things. It motivates us to resolve conflict instead of holding on to grudges. It inspires us to share our feelings, knowing that we may not be able to do it later. It helps us guard against procrastination. It encourages us to think hard about our priorities, to decide what's immediately important. And it focuses our attention on God, the Source and Sustainer of life. He knows exactly how many days we'll spend in this world—and how we can make the most of every one of them.

God, thank You for reminding me how essential it is to make the most of today. When life gets busy, it's tempting to postpone important things until another day. It's also tempting to assume that I have plenty of time to do the things I need–and want–to do. But I know all too well that that's not always the case–that tomorrow is guaranteed to no one. So help me prioritize the things that are truly important. Give me the focus and perseverance to accomplish what I need to do today.

AMEN.

KNOW YOUR STRENGTH

I can do all things through him who strengthens me.

PHILIPPIANS 4:13 ESV

You've probably heard stories of people who performed near-superhuman feats in times of extreme crisis. When lives were on the line, ordinary folks found strength and courage they didn't know they had to lift automobiles, run into burning buildings, or brave rip currents. Philippians 4:13 says that kind of strength and courage is available in spiritual form as well. "I can do all things" is a bold statement—and one that covers a lot of ground. "All things" might include finally making a life-altering decision that you've been putting off—and feeling peace about it. Or overcoming a habit you've been wrestling with for too long. Or stepping into a role that you're not entirely comfortable with. Whatever the case, we must remember that the boldness that makes these things possible is available only "through him who strengthens" us. The credit for everything we accomplish with that strength belongs to God alone.

God, thank You for this boost of confidence from Your Word. How often do I put unnecessary limits on my potential, based on an inaccurate self-evaluation? How often do I underestimate what I'm truly capable of? Show me how to claim the promise of Philippians 4:13. Open my eyes to the broad scope of things I can accomplish, if I rely on Your strength. Show me how to heal a relationship that I thought was damaged beyond repair. Or quit something I've been struggling with for a long time. Or learn to see myself the way You see me. I know I can't do these things on my own.

IF YOU HELP ME ACCOMPLISH THEM, I WILL GIVE YOU ALL THE CREDIT. AMEN.

SAVED BY GRACE

For you are saved by grace through faith,
and this is not from yourselves;
it is God's gift—not from works,
so that no one can boast.

EPHESIANS 2:8–9 CSB

What's the best gift you ever received? What did it cost? Not just in terms of price, but also in sacrifice and effort. A gift doesn't have to be expensive to be precious. Its cost can be measured by what the giver invested in it. Think of a father giving up his evenings and weekends to build a treehouse for his son. Or a wife who plans every detail of an unforgettable surprise party for her husband. The gift Paul talks about in Ephesians 2 is far beyond any other. God gave us a gift that cost Him what was most precious to Him: His only Son. It was the only way to give us eternal life. His motivation was pure love. We don't deserve His gift. His grace makes it possible. All we have to do is accept it.

God, thank You for Your amazing grace.
You treat me with a goodness that I don't deserve.
You sacrificed what was most precious to You
for my sake. I can't imagine a greater gift.
No words can adequately thank You for such
a gift, but that won't stop me from trying–again
and again. Thank You for loving me so much
that You sent Your Son to take the punishment
for my wrongdoing and die in my place.
Thank You for doing what I can't do:
providing a way for me to be saved from the
eternal punishment I deserve for my sin and
making it possible for me to live forever with You.

AMEN.

PUT ON THE ARMOR OF GOD

Put on all the armor that God gives you, so that you will be able to stand up against the Devil's evil tricks.

EPHESIANS 6:11 GNT

The war is over. Jesus defeated the devil once and for all when He completed God's plan of salvation. And when God's judgment day comes, the devil will be punished forever. Until that time, however, he's free to wage battle against God's people. His goal is to weaken and destroy our Christian faith. His weapons include doubt, temptation, and lies. The moment we put our trust in Jesus, we become Satan's enemy. The more we grow in our faith, through prayer, Bible study, and spending time with other believers, the more of a threat we become to him. And the more intense his attacks become. But God won't let us face him unprotected. He equips us with spiritual "armor," made up of His Word, His truth, His peace, and our faith, among other things. The devil is powerless against them. If we learn how to use each piece of armor, we can win any spiritual battle.

God, thank You first for Your plan of salvation that defeated the devil once and for all. Thank You for Your assurance that Your enemy will face eternal punishment for the evil he has done. Thank You for the warnings in Your Word about the danger he still poses. Give me a sense of how to respond to that danger. Show me how to be wary of the devil without being afraid of him. Help me recognize what spiritual battle looks like. I know that the devil's goal is to weaken my faith, but I can't always recognize his attacks.

SHOW ME HOW TO USE YOUR ARMOR TO PROTECT MYSELF.

AMEN.

STAY COURAGEOUS

Be strong and courageous. Do not be afraid or terrified because of them, for the Lord your God goes with you; He will never leave you nor forsake you.

DEUTERONOMY 31:6 NIV

If you hold your thumb directly in front of your face when you look up at the sky, you can blot out the sun, even though the sun is billions of times bigger than your thumb. It's simply a matter of perspective. Things that are close to you seem much larger than they really are. The same principle applies to your problems and fears. Because they're constantly in your thoughts, they loom larger than they really are. From certain perspectives, they can even temporarily blot out your view of God. This verse from Deuteronomy is like a corrective lens. It lets you see God—and any potential problems you may face—in the proper perspective. The ability to be strong and courageous in the face of adversity comes from the realization that you're not facing it alone. God goes before you. He knows exactly what you need to overcome the fear, anxiety, obstacles, and problems in your path. And He will supply it—every day of your life.

God, You are bigger and more powerful than any problem I will ever face. If I ever start to doubt that, it's because my perspective is off. You make it possible for me to be strong and courageous. Thank You for Your promise to always go with me and never leave me. Forgive me for the times I let my fears get the best of me. Give me the courage to step out of my comfort zone, knowing that You will be beside me every step of the way.

AND REMIND ME TO GIVE YOU ALL THE CREDIT FOR MY COURAGE.

AMEN.

A COMMUNITY OF FAITH

And let's consider how to encourage one another in love and good deeds, not abandoning our own meeting together, as is the habit of some people, but encouraging one another; and all the more as you see the day drawing near.

HEBREWS 10:24–25 NASB

Good things happen when you spend time with people who love and follow Jesus. They share a profound common experience. They've had their lives transformed by Jesus. They've had an inner joy and hope ignited within them, something that even the worst of circumstances can't douse. When Christians get together, their joy and hope bubble to the surface and become something greater than the sum of their parts. The spirit of community and shared experience among Christians allows you to forge some deep connections. When you spend time with Christians, you discover that your personal struggles aren't unique to you. You find that others are struggling too. You feel comfortable opening up about those struggles. You feel embraced, not rejected. You find people who want the best for you. You find people who see potential in you that you may not even be aware of.

God, thank You for making the life of faith a shared experience. Thank You for the unique bond of friendship that develops between those who love and follow Jesus. Please bring people into my life who understand where I am, spiritually speaking. People who can empathize with my struggles. People who can give me encouragement and guidance. Show me, too, how I can make a difference in other people's lives. Show me how to encourage others and inspire them to do good things. Help me find a church home where I feel comfortable, accepted, and embraced. Help me experience the kind of community described in Hebrews 10.

AMEN.

WALK BY FAITH

Trust in the LORD with all your heart,
and lean not on your own understanding;
in all your ways acknowledge Him,
and He shall direct your paths.

PROVERBS 3:5–6 NKJV

Many of us were born with a DIY mindset. We'll defer to experts in certain areas, like brain surgery or major plumbing projects. But for the most part, we prefer to trust our own skills and abilities. We prefer to navigate our way through life on our own. In the context of this passage, though, that approach doesn't make sense. Because no matter how keen our understanding of the world is, it's no match for God's. God knows where every path leads. He can steer us away from risky detours and dead ends. He can lead us to people, places, and situations that change us forever, for the better. We can trust Him because He loves us and wants only what's best for us. We honor Him when we acknowledge His wisdom and trustworthiness. We glorify Him when we turn the reins of our lives over to Him. God never steers anyone wrong.

God, thank You for Your promise to direct my paths. You know how tempting it is to try to be self-sufficient. To live by my own wits. To carve my own path through life. Help me resist those temptations. Show me the limits of my understanding. Save me from overconfidence in my own abilities. Give me the wisdom to trust Your wisdom, which is never wrong. You know all things because You created and control all things. No path is a mystery to You. Let me never lose sight of those truths. Help me learn to lean on You, instead of my own understanding.

AMEN.

LEARN TO WORSHIP

Come, let us worship and bow down.
Let us kneel before the Lord our maker.

PSALM 95:6 NLT

A person who struggles with chronic pain might schedule regular chiropractic appointments to align the body. Precise physical adjustments often provide relief. But the wear and tear of daily life can throw the body out of alignment again. Hence, the need for regular appointments. Think of worship as a spiritual chiropractic appointment. God created us with a specific spiritual alignment. That alignment begins with acknowledging who He is and what He does. We were created to stand in awe of our Creator. To be amazed and humbled by His love, grace, wisdom, power, mercy, and forgiveness. Worship gives us a chance to align ourselves spiritually by celebrating God in song, humbling ourselves in prayer, and allowing His Word to guide our lives. Like the physical alignment of a chiropractor, however, the spiritual alignment of worship is temporary. The temptations of daily life—to ignore God, to give priority to our own desires—throw us out of spiritual alignment. That's why the Bible places such a high priority on frequent, purposeful worship.

God, I am in awe of You. I am surrounded by Your beauty, the work of Your creation. You alone deserve my worship and praise. Thank You for creating me spiritually aligned with You. Guide my efforts to worship You in a meaningful way. Help me understand the depths of Your love, grace, wisdom, power, mercy, and forgiveness so that I can celebrate You more. Remind me to come to You often–every day–for spiritual alignment. Make me always sensitive to my need for Your presence and Your Word so that I will prioritize worship.

AMEN.

BE AN ENCOURAGER

Let no corrupting talk come out of your mouths, but only such as is good for building up, as fits the occasion, that it may give grace to those who hear.

EPHESIANS 4:29 ESV

Think of this verse as a quick tutorial on how to become an effective influencer—not necessarily on social media, but in real life. It highlights four things you can do to make a lasting impact on friends, loved ones, and new acquaintances alike. These simple actions also help others see Jesus's influence in your life. First, put an end to negative talk, including gossip and offensive jokes. Set a higher standard for yourself. Second, find ways to work sincere praise and encouragement into your interactions. Try to make people feel good about themselves when they're with you. Third, fit the occasion. Think hard about what to say—and what not to say—in specific situations. Fourth, give grace. Be quick to forgive and slow to anger. Remember, we're all works in progress.

God, thank You for the people in my life who build me up. Thank You for the people who find the right words to say at the right time. Thank You for the people who have shown me what grace looks like. Let me learn from their example. Give me the discipline to corral my negative talk. Help me set a higher bar for myself in terms of what comes out of my mouth. Guide my attempts to praise and encourage. Show me how to say things that make people feel better. Sharpen my sense of timing. Show me how to uplift people when they need it most. Help me be quick to forgive and slow to anger, just like You.

AMEN.

BUILD A STRONG FOUNDATION

"Therefore, everyone who hears these words of Mine and acts on them will be like a wise man who built his house on the rock. The rain fell, the rivers rose, and the winds blew and pounded that house. Yet it didn't collapse, because its foundation was on the rock."

MATTHEW 7:24-25 CSB

Whether we realize it or not, we all build our lives on some kind of foundation. For example, we might build on a foundation of money. We might convince ourselves that wealth, or at least financial security, will bring us happiness, give meaning to our lives, and ultimately fulfill our needs. We would then make decisions primarily with an eye on our bottom line. We would measure success by the size of our investment portfolio. Or we might build our lives on foundations of pleasure, achievement, or popularity. It's only when life's storms blow in that we realize how unstable our foundation is. Money can be lost. Pleasures are fleeting. Achievements are a never-ending pursuit. Popularity is fickle. That's why Jesus says build your life on something solid. Build it on the truths found in God's Word.

God, thank You for this warning in Your Word. It would be a terrible thing to find out too late that I'd built my life on something that will collapse. Show me how to build my life on the foundation of Your Word. Help me understand what Your promises and commands look like when they're put into action. Show me how to place them at the center of everything I do so that they can support me. Thank You for giving me a foundation I can trust when life's storms get intense.

LET ME NEVER LOSE SIGHT OF YOUR STRENGTH AND PROTECTION.

AMEN.

PRACTICE PATIENCE

Be patient, then, my friends, until the Lord comes.
See how patient farmers are as they wait
for their land to produce precious crops.
They wait patiently for the autumn and spring rains.
You also must be patient. Keep your hopes high,
for the day of the Lord's coming is near.

JAMES 5:7–8 GNT

Patience is love in action. First Corinthians 13 is known as the "love chapter" of the Bible. In it, Paul lists the qualities of the love that God shows us—and the love He asks us to show one another. At the very top of his list? "Love is patient" (I Corinthians 13:4). God shows His patience for us by delaying His coming judgment. In the meantime, He forgives us every time we're genuinely sorry for something we've done that was wrong. He comforts us every time we feel anxious. He encourages us every time we start to doubt. And He doesn't get tired of doing it. That's patience—and love—in action. In return, we honor God by acknowledging that His plan and His timing are perfect and deserve to be trusted.

God, thank You for being patient with me. I try to live in a way that pleases You, but I often fall short. And every time I do, You forgive me. You never get tired of comforting me, encouraging me, and giving me direction. If people ask how I know You love me, I can point to Your patience. Give me the wisdom and perspective to follow Your example. There are times when I desperately want You to intervene in a situation.

REMIND ME THAT I HONOR YOU EVERY TIME I STAY PATIENT AND TRUST YOUR TIMING.

AMEN.

FOREVER HOPE

"And if I go and prepare a place for you, I will come back and take you to be with Me that you also may be where I am."

JOHN 14:3 NIV

Jesus had just informed His disciples that His earthly ministry was coming to an end. In a very short time, the events leading to His death would commence. His disciples were understandably shaken by the news. In this verse, Jesus turns their eyes away from the present to the future. The separation is only temporary, He emphasizes. Soon they will be together forever. He's talking not just to the disciples in the room but to everyone who follows Him. Only Jesus can offer these assurances because only He can make them possible. Jesus fulfilled His part in making eternal life a reality. He lived a sinless life, died to take the punishment for our sins, and rose from the dead. We fulfill our part by waiting patiently, trusting in Him, and looking forward to an unimaginably joyous eternity. His words in this verse allow us to remain hopeful, no matter how hopeless things seem. We're able to say with confidence, "I have something amazing waiting for me."

God, thank You for the promise of eternal life. The words that Jesus spoke to His disciples two thousand years ago have lost none of their reliability. Thank You for giving me something rock-solid to hold on to when doubts arise. I can only imagine the results of Jesus's preparations, but I know they will be amazing. Thank You for including me in Your eternal plans. Give me the wisdom to keep eternity in perspective–to draw courage and hope from what awaits without losing sight of what I need to do here.

AMEN.

BEAR FRUIT

But the fruit of the Spirit is love, joy, peace, patience, kindness, goodness, faithfulness, gentleness, self-control; against such things there is no law.

GALATIANS 5:22-23 NASB

Research suggests that, over time, spouses become more and more alike. The process is known as "the chameleon effect." Husbands and wives unconsciously adopt each other's behaviors, speaking styles, facial expressions, and body language. Familiarity doesn't always breed contempt; sometimes it breeds imitation. A similar thing happens when you get to know Jesus. The more time you spend learning about Him, thinking about the way He lived and the things He said, the more His attributes start to show up in your life. That's what the fruit of the Spirit is: evidence of Jesus's impact on your life. You may find that you're more purposeful in showing love to others. Or that you feel joy when, logically, you shouldn't. Or that you don't lose control as quickly when you're triggered. You will notice Jesus's impact on you—and so will others.

God, thank You for the amazing transformation that You make possible. Thank You for allowing Jesus's attributes to infiltrate my life. His love helps me show genuine compassion to others. His joy gives me contentment, regardless of my circumstances. His peace gives me an inner calm in stressful times. His patience helps me interact with people in a productive way. His kindness inspires me to show mercy. His goodness helps me make decisions that are morally right. His faithfulness makes me reliable. His gentleness keeps me from hurting others with my words. His self-control helps me resist temptation. Let the fruit of the Spirit blossom in my life so that I can make a difference in the lives of others and point them to You.

AMEN.

GOD IS PATIENT

The Lord is not slack concerning His promise,
as some count slackness, but is longsuffering toward us,
not willing that any should perish
but that all should come to repentance.

II PETER 3:9 NKJV

One of the biggest hurdles many people face in understanding God is the overwhelming presence of evil in the world. Why doesn't God do something about corrupt leaders, vicious criminals, and people who prey on others? In other words, why don't bad people get what's coming to them? It's not because God doesn't care—or that He's powerless to do anything about it. It's because He cares so much that He's holding back His power—at least, for a while. What seems like unnecessary delay to us is actually God's plan to give people as much time as possible to turn away from evil and escape His coming judgment. He's not a vengeful God who can't wait to execute judgment. He's a loving God who doesn't want anyone to face His wrath. God's judgment will come. His perfect justice demands it. Before it does, though, He's giving people time to repent and be saved from it.

God, thank You for the promises in Your Word—and for always being faithful to them. Your promise to deal with evil once and for all gives me comfort because I know I can trust You. Sometimes it may seem that bad people prosper, and that can be discouraging. But I trust Your perfect timing. And I'm in awe of Your patience. You love people so much that You're willing to postpone Your judgment so that as many as possible can turn to You. Thank You for being patient with me. Help me trust Your timing in showing patience to others. Help me align my sense of justice with Your sense of mercy.

AMEN.

CELEBRATE FORGIVENESS

"Even if that person wrongs you seven times a day and each time turns again and asks forgiveness, you must forgive."

LUKE 17:4 NLT

Jesus understood the power of forgiveness to change lives—not just of the people who receive it, but also of the people who offer it. The power to forgive is one of the things we have in common with God. It's part of our being created in His image. Every time we forgive, as He forgives, we glorify Him and grow closer to Him. Forgiveness is also important to our mental health. Resentment, bitterness, and grudges occupy a huge emotional bandwidth. They leave little room for healthy feelings. Forgiveness allows us to release those negative emotions before they take root. Forgiveness clears our conscience. It allows us to walk away from conflict without having to worry about whether we should have done something differently. Forgiveness helps protect and restore relationships. It's hard for other people to hold a grudge against us when we refuse to do the same. Forgiveness is one of the greatest gifts we can give others—and ourselves.

God, thank You for forgiving me—not once, not seven times, but every time I sincerely ask You to. Your love for me is amazing. You know what guilt can do to my physical, spiritual, and emotional health, so You free me from it. You forgive me completely. You wipe my slate clean. And You give me the strength to do the same for others. Help me understand how freeing it is to let go of grudges, instead of holding on to them and nursing them over time. Let me live with no malice in my heart toward anyone.

LET ME SHOW OTHERS THE FORGIVENESS YOU'VE SHOWN ME. AMEN.

EVERYONE WELCOME

For in one Spirit we were all baptized into one body—
Jews or Greeks, slaves or free—
and all were made to drink of one Spirit."

I CORINTHIANS 12:13 ESV

On paper, the church described in the Bible shouldn't work. "Jews or Greeks, slaves or free" covers too wide a swath of demographics. The stark differences between people's cultural backgrounds, economic status, political affiliation, lifestyles, ambitions, priorities, and personalities seem to leave little room for common ground. Yet that's the church God designed. Diversity is embedded in its DNA. The fact that it *does* function is evidence of God's handiwork. The church is greater than the sum of its parts because God integrates those parts into something unique—something special. God welcomes everyone into His church because every person brings a unique life experience and point of view that adds to the church's viability. When you find a church, you find a place where you're not only welcome but needed. You find a place where you belong and matter.

God, thank You for welcoming everyone. Thank You for creating a spiritual body—the church—that is made up of such diverse members. Help me find my place in a local body of believers. You have created a group that's made up not just of people from different backgrounds but also of people with different skills and abilities. Help me recognize my own gifts—what I can contribute to the body. Show me how I can work with people who are different from me. Give me the courage to stand with the diverse people who are part of the body. Guide me through the process of finding a church home, a place where I'm welcome and can grow in my Christian faith.

AMEN.

TRUST THAT EVIL WILL BE PUNISHED

For the wrongdoer will be paid back for whatever wrong he has done, and there is no favoritism.

COLOSSIANS 3:25 CSB

Genesis 1:27 says God created man in His own image. One way in which God's image can be seen in us is our desire for justice. Most of us, when we see someone do something wrong, instinctively root for the person to face consequences. If those consequences don't occur, we react—with outrage, anger, or cynicism, depending on our personality. This verse reminds us where our desire for justice comes from. God is just. His nature demands that all wrongdoers face appropriate consequences. The problem is, our view of justice is imperfect. Our emotions get in the way. We allow prejudice and favoritism to color our perspective. We demand instant gratification. Sometimes we even give in to the temptation to dispense our own payback. God's justice, in contrast, is perfect. His timing is perfect. His consequences are perfect—never too harsh, never too lenient. We can trust Him to punish wrongdoers.

God, thank You for taking justice out of my hands. If it were up to me, I might let my emotions get the better of me. I might be tempted to take an eye for an eye. And instead of resolving conflict, I would only make things worse. So thank You for showing me a better way. Help me let go of my demands for personal justice. Give me the patience to wait for justice from You because Your timing is perfect. Help me be satisfied with the consequences You think are appropriate.

HELP ME RECOGNIZE YOUR WISDOM AND GRACE IN DEALING WITH WRONGDOERS.

AMEN.

LET YOUR LIGHT SHINE

"You are like light for the whole world.
A city built on a hill cannot be hid.
No one lights a lamp and puts it under a bowl;
instead it is put on the lampstand,
where it gives light for everyone in the house.
In the same way your light must shine before people,
so that they will see the good things you do
and praise your Father in heaven."

MATTHEW 5:14–16 GNT

The moon generates no light of its own. The light that seems to come from the moon is reflected sunlight. In the same way, the light that Jesus talks about in Matthew 5 isn't generated by His followers. The light that seems to come from them is actually reflected light from Jesus. Jesus transforms lives, gives hope, and promises that we will live forever. He gives us purpose, strength, encouragement, and guidance. He makes us feel loved—unconditionally and sacrificially. Those changes are apparent in the people who follow Him. His nature is reflected in us. Instead of trying to hide or downplay those radical changes in our lives, Jesus says let everyone see them. Give other people a glimpse of what Jesus is capable of doing.

God, thank You for giving us light and hope. The world can be a dark place sometimes. People long for the kind of hope, assurance, purpose, strength, encouragement, guidance, and love that Jesus offers, but they don't always know where to look for it. Jesus's instructions in Matthew 5 solve that problem. I want Jesus's light to shine through me. Show me how to make that happen.

GIVE ME THE COURAGE TO REPRESENT JESUS AND SHOW OTHERS WHERE LIGHT CAN BE FOUND.

AMEN.

SPEAK UP

Preach the word; be prepared in season and out of season; correct, rebuke and encourage— with great patience and careful instruction.

II TIMOTHY 4:2 NIV

Could you change a tire on the side of a highway if you had to? Could you whip up an impromptu breakfast for unexpected guests? Both are useful skills to have in a pinch. Paul, the Christian leader who wrote 2 Timothy, adds another. Could you share God's message with other people? Could you explain what it means to follow Jesus? Could you play the role of mentor, correcting, rebuking, and encouraging as needed? There's wisdom in becoming a "spiritual first responder." You never know when you'll have opportunities to talk about your Christian faith, so it's important to be prepared when those opportunities arise. You don't have to be a theologian or a minister to "preach the word." You just need to be able to share your own experience. Though you may know only a little about God's Word right now, you may find that it's exactly enough to make a difference in someone's life.

God, thank You for the people in my life who taught me about Your Word. Thank You for the people who corrected me when I was wrong. Thank You for the people who rebuked me when I was out of line. Thank You for the people who encouraged me along the way. Please help me play a similar role in other people's lives. Give me the courage and sensitivity to correct and rebuke people in a loving way. Make me aware of opportunities to encourage. Guide my words so that they will have maximum impact.

HELP ME LEARN YOUR WORD AND BECOME COMFORTABLE IN TALKING ABOUT IT WITH OTHERS. AMEN.

MEMORIZE GOD'S WORD

I have treasured Your word in my heart,
so that I may not sin against You."

PSALM 119:11 NASB

Do you collect anything? Baseball cards? Coins? Autographs? If you do, you can appreciate the spirit of this verse. God doesn't want you to just read the Bible; He wants you to collect its wisdom. You do that by running verses through your mind again and again until they stick in your memory. Look for passages that speak to the situations you're facing, passages that challenge, comfort, or encourage you. Treat them like the valuable, but practical, treasures they are. Practice using them in different situations. If you're feeling anxious, repeat, "Cast all your anxiety on Him, because He cares about you" (I Peter 5:7 NASB). If you're tempted to fall back into an old habit, remind yourself, "God is faithful, so He will not allow you to be tempted beyond what you are able" (I Corinthians 10:13 NASB). God's Word is different from most other treasures in that its value increases every time you use it.

Father, thank You for the treasure You give us in Your Word. Thank You for revealing Yourself in it so that I can get to know You. Thank You for putting into writing the things You want me to do and the things You want me to avoid. Thank You for filling the pages of Your Word with hope. Thank You for showing me how to be joyful in all circumstances. Thank You for revealing Your will for my life. Thank You for lighting the paths You want me to take. Help me store the wisdom of Your Word in my heart and memory so that I can use it as often as necessary.

AMEN.

CELEBRATE TRIBULATION?

And not only that, but we also glory in tribulations, knowing that tribulation produces perseverance; and perseverance, character; and character, hope.

ROMANS 5:3–4 NKJV

If you've ever trained for a marathon, you know the agony of the first long run. Aching muscles, nausea, cramps, exhaustion, and mental fatigue are just some of the signs that you're taking a huge step. At that point, you're faced with a choice. You can embrace the pain and suffering, knowing that you're growing stronger, increasing your endurance, and getting mentally tougher with every step. Or you can stop, limp home, and attend the marathon as a spectator. This passage from Romans presents a similar spiritual scenario. Tribulations are inevitable in life. Some push us to our absolute limit. We can choose to give up when we reach that point—or we can embrace the challenges they bring, because tribulations test us in unique ways. They offer opportunities to build perseverance, character, strength, perspective, and faith that can last a lifetime. Tribulations allow us to experience God's amazing love and protection firsthand. And they leave hope in their wake because we get a sense of what we're capable of overcoming.

God, thank You for bringing something good from something bad. Thank You for standing with me in every tribulation. Not only do You keep me from being beaten down by it, but You also provide a way for me grow and thrive in the midst of it. Remind me as often as necessary that good things come from tribulations. Open my eyes to the perseverance, character, strength, perspective, and faith that you're building in me.

GIVE ME THE PERSPECTIVE TO FACE TRIBULATIONS WITH CONFIDENCE AND OPTIMISM. AMEN.

"WHO DO YOU SAY I AM?"

Then He asked them, "But who do you say I am?" Simon Peter answered, "You are the Messiah, the Son of the living God."

MATTHEW 16:15–16 NLT

Certain questions require a carefully considered response. "Do you take this woman to be your lawfully wedded wife?" "Do you know why I pulled you over?" "Dad, where do babies come from?" But no question compares in importance to the one Jesus asks in this passage: *Who do you say I am?* There's no shortage of opinions. Some say He was a great teacher. Others say He was a social revolutionary. But only one answer unlocks eternal life, and that's the one Peter gave. Peter said, in essence, *You are the Savior that God promised the world. You are God's Son. You are the only path to eternal life. You are the way, the truth, and the life. No one comes to the Father except through You*. That was Peter's statement of belief. He backed up his words with his actions. He devoted his life to following Jesus. And if you do the same, you can be assured of eternal life and enjoy a personal relationship with God as well.

God, I am ready to answer Jesus's question. I say He is the Savior. He came to earth to live a sinless life so that He could be the perfect sacrifice. His death paid the price that Your holiness and justice demanded for the world's sins. He then conquered death by rising from the grave, making it possible for everyone who believes in Him to have eternal life. I believe in Him. I know I can do nothing to save myself so I must rely on Jesus's sacrifice.

FORGIVE ME FOR MY SINS
AND MAKE ME RIGHTEOUS
IN YOUR EYES.
AMEN.

RECRUIT WISE COUNSELORS

Where there is no guidance, a people falls,
but in an abundance of counselors there is safety.

PROVERBS 11:14 ESV

If you were going to build a house, how many people would you involve in the process? Your group might include an architect, a general contractor, a dozen or more subcontractors, an interior designer, a landscaper, and more. To do it right, you'd want to find the right people to consult. Doesn't it make sense to take the same approach to building your life? That's the point of this verse from Proverbs. God has put in your orbit people who can help you live the life He intends. People who possess hard-earned wisdom that you need to hear. People who have experienced God's extraordinary blessings and can show you where they're found. People who can point to danger areas they know all too well. People who have expertise in areas where you're a novice. People who understand how to grow and mature in the Christian life. It's up to you to recruit them as counselors and follow their guidance.

Father, thank You for the people who have guided and encouraged me. Their voices are part of the soundtrack of my life. You brought them into my orbit because You care about me. You don't want to see me fall. I know that I would not be the person I am today without their influence, which You made possible. Give me the wisdom to recognize other potential mentors. Help me weigh their input against the truth of Your Word. Give me opportunities to show all my counselors my deepest gratitude.

AND PLEASE GIVE ME THE CHANCE TO SERVE AS A COUNSELOR TO OTHERS IN NEED. AMEN.

GLORIFY GOD

So, whether you eat or drink, or whatever you do, do everything for the glory of God.

I CORINTHIANS 10:31 CSB

What's the secret to a joyous, fulfilling, and meaningful life? Ask one hundred different people, and you'll probably get one hundred different answers. But you could boil it down to these seven words: *Do everything for the glory of God*. That involves trying to mirror His image, follow the commands in His Word, love others as He does, and help others see in Him what we do. There is no higher calling and no greater satisfaction than accomplishing this. You always have two sets of witnesses to the things you do. The first is God, who sees everything. The second is other people, who see only what you do in public. Every time you make a God-honoring choice in private, God is pleased, because You're glorifying Him in the way you live. Every time you make a similar choice in public, you draw other people's attention to Him and His influence in Your life. Once again, He's glorified. Doing everything for the glory of God, then, is an absolute win-win.

Father, thank You for showing me that to have a joyous, fulfilling, and meaningful life, I need to do everything for Your glory. Thank You for giving me the chance to honor You in everything I do. Open my eyes to the opportunities I have every day to bring glory to You through the choices I make. Guide my decision-making. Help me recognize how various decisions will reflect on You. Show me Your will so that I can choose it.

REMIND ME TO DIRECT
ALL PRAISE AND GLORY TO YOU.
AMEN.

LOVE ONE ANOTHER

"If you have love for one another, then everyone will know that you are My disciples."

JOHN 13:35 GNT

Certain people are easy to pick out of a crowd. Military personnel carry themselves in a recognizable way. Parents of young children can be identified by their watchful eyes. Introverts usually can be spotted away from the action. Jesus wants His followers to be counted among these easily recognizable groups. And He wants love—genuine, sacrificial, obvious love—to be the dead giveaway. Christians are a diverse lot. Aside from our shared devotion to Jesus, we have little to connect us. So the existence of a deep, binding love among us signals something extraordinary in our lives. Something that can only be explained by the transformation Jesus brings about. People who are looking to fill a void in their own lives are especially drawn to the love believers have for one another. The love Jesus requires from His followers impacts not only us but also everyone who witnesses it. And the result is countless changed lives.

God, thank You for placing love at the center of everything You do. Thank You for challenging believers to love another in life-changing ways. Thank You for the privilege of identifying as one of Jesus's disciples. Give me a sense of what the love described in this verse should look like in my own life. Ignite a spark of compassion and concern in me so that I can show genuine love to other people in my church and community. Let me never take those relationships for granted. You love me, generously and sacrificially. And when I show generous, sacrificial love to others, people see the work of Jesus in me.

THANK YOU FOR GIVING ME A PLACE IN YOUR CHAIN OF LOVE.

AMEN.

A NEW YOU

Therefore, if anyone is in Christ, the new creation has come: The old has gone, the new is here!

II CORINTHIANS 5:17 NIV

If high school reunions teach us anything, it's that everyone changes—in physical appearance, personality, outlook on life, and other ways. Chances are, you can pinpoint more than a few differences between the person you used to be and the person you are now. While some of those changes may be dramatic, they're not total. You can still see and hear traces of the old person. There's still something familiar in there. A person who believes in Jesus, on the other hand, undergoes a complete spiritual transformation. He becomes a new person entirely, in God's eyes. When God looks at him, He no longer sees the man's old self. He no longer holds the man accountable for his old wrongs. As a new person, the man is no longer controlled by his worst instincts. His new nature gives him the ability to resist temptation, to understand and apply God's wisdom, and to live in a way that inspires others. His new nature secures for him a place in God's family and makes eternal life possible.

God, thank You for the opportunity to start over. Forgive me for the things I've done wrong. I believe that Jesus sacrificed His life so that everyone who trusts in Him may have eternal life. I believe in Him. I put my trust in Him. I want to be a new creation. Give me a fresh start. Break the power of temptation over me. Help me understand what Your Word says and apply it to my life. Let others see the difference in me.

THANK YOU FOR MAKING IT POSSIBLE FOR ME TO KNOW WHERE I WILL GO AFTER I DIE. AMEN.

USE YOUR TIME WISELY

So be careful how you live.
Don't live like ignorant people, but like wise people.
Make good use of every opportunity you have,
because these are evil days. Don't be fools, then,
but try to find out what the Lord wants you to do.

EPHESIANS 5:15–17 GNT

Every new day brings a fresh twenty-four hours to spend as we choose. This passage encourages us to make the most of those hours. And for good reason. If you follow Jesus, God is going to open all kinds of opportunities for you. That's a given. So why not live in a way that prepares you for those opportunities? You may have no idea what they will be, but you can learn to spot them when they come. You do that by reading God's Word. By discovering His promises in it. By looking at the opportunities He opened for people in it. You can do it by praying. By asking God to help you recognize His direction for your life. And you can do it by making daily decisions based on what you think would please God.

God, thank You for a fresh twenty-four hours to live. I don't want to take that time for granted. Give me the perspective I need to make the most of the hours You give me. Teach me to tell the difference between what ultimately matters and what doesn't. Thank You for the opportunities on my horizon. I may not know what they are, but I know I can trust You. I know that they will serve a greater purpose. Help me prepare for what You have in store for me.

WHEN A DOOR OPENS,
LET ME BE READY
TO WALK THROUGH IT.
AMEN.

A LITTLE HELP WITH YOUR PRAYERS

Likewise the Spirit also helps in our weaknesses. For we do not know what we should pray for as we ought, but the Spirit Himself makes intercession for us with groanings which cannot be uttered.

ROMANS 8:26 NKJV

An ancient Greek saying advises, "Know thyself." While that may sound like easy advice to follow, it's actually quite difficult. To know ourselves completely, we must delve into areas we prefer to keep hidden. We must look past our carefully constructed facades to the real person underneath. We must search for blind spots we're not aware of. Yet that's exactly what God wants us to do when we pray. He wants us to open every part of ourselves to Him—so much so that if we can't do it, He will do it for us. He will make the hidden things in us known. He places such a high priority on prayer that He will work both sides of the conversation until we're able to communicate transparently with Him.

God, thank You for placing such a high priority on my time with You. Thank You for keeping the lines of communication open even when I don't know what to say. Thank You for knowing and loving me so completely that You can finish my prayers for me. I may not always pray wisely. I may start some prayers before I know exactly what to pray for. I may occasionally focus on insignificant details and lose sight of the big picture. Sometimes I may allow my own self-interests to influence my prayers. But I want to get better. I want my prayers to make a difference. Help me learn how to do that. Until I do, thank You for interceding for me and making my prayers acceptable to You.

AMEN.

A FRIEND INDEED

A friend is always loyal,
and a brother is born to help in time of need.

PROVERBS 17:17 NLT

Genuine friendship is a trial by fire. When times are good, you probably have no shortage of family members, coworkers, classmates, neighbors, teammates, and casual acquaintances that you call friends. But the real test of friendship comes when life turns dark. If you're struggling—physically, emotionally, relationally, financially—look around. The people who are standing with you are the keepers. The ones who reach out when you withdraw. The ones who show up when you need help. The ones who refuse to give up on you. The ones who are motivated only by your best interests. The ones who know better when you say you're fine. The ones who stay loyal long after it's convenient or easy to do so. Those friends are God's gifts to you. Of course, friendship is a two-way street. If you prove your willingness to go through the fire with your friends, you are God's gift to them.

God, thank You for the genuine friends You've brought into my life. Thank You for the people who stand by me, in good times and bad. Thank You for the love, support, comfort, and encouragement I receive from them. I would not be the man I am today without them. Help me be a loyal friend to others. Give me the courage to stand with my friends when things turn dark. Help me see past the surface of their lives to their real emotions. Make me aware of their needs. Show me the role they need me to fill. Help me become the kind of friend Proverbs 17 talks about. Help me become a role model of loyalty to the people in my life.

AMEN.

KEEP YOUR GUARD UP

Be sober-minded; be watchful. Your adversary the devil prowls around like a roaring lion, seeking someone to devour.

I PETER 5:8 ESV

When a boxer or MMA fighter faces off against an opponent in the ring, he looks for the smallest wrong move, a split-second relaxing of defenses. When he sees vulnerability, he attacks, quickly and fiercely. Spiritually speaking, that's what the devil does too. As God's enemy, he works to prevent God's work from being done by attacking people who do it. He can't wait to hit you with doubt, lust, temptation, guilt, anything that will knock you off your game. All he needs is the slightest opening. A moment of weakness. An impulsive return to an old habit. An encounter with the wrong person. A careless remark. When he sees vulnerability, he pounces, quickly and viciously. His goal is to knock you out spiritually, to keep you from building a strong relationship with God. He's a formidable opponent, but he's no match for God, who's in your corner. If you stay close to God and aware of the devil's strategy, you have nothing to fear.

God, thank You for showing me my enemy's fight strategy. Thank You for stepping into the ring with me. Knowing that I have an enemy who's constantly looking for an opening to attack is scary. But knowing that I can depend on You to guide me through my fight is a huge relief. Show me the areas where I'm vulnerable and help me strengthen them. Help me understand what the devil is trying to do to my life and how I can prevent him from succeeding.

GIVE ME THE STRENGTH AND ENDURANCE I NEED FOR THE FIGHT.

AMEN.

RENEW YOUR STRENGTH

But those who trust in the Lord renew their strength; they will soar on wings like eagles; they will run and not become weary, they will walk and not faint.

ISAIAH 40:31 CSB

Sometimes life feels like one continual test of strength—a challenge to see how much we can bear physically, mentally, emotionally, and spiritually. Sometimes the test requires only light lifting—finding the motivation to finish a chore, for example. Other times it requires some heavy lifting, but only for a short time. A fender bender, an argument with a loved one, and a work deadline all require more than a little exertion. But if those events are spaced out far enough, they don't feel overwhelming. Some parts of the test, however, call for every bit of strength we have—and then some. Aging parents, financial difficulties, mental health struggles, and other circumstances that seem to have no end in sight can overwhelm us. In this verse from Isaiah, God says if we're trying to lift these things on our own, we're doing it wrong. The right way is to give every strength test to Him and let Him do the heavy lifting.

God, thank You for Your amazing promise. Thank You for never giving me more than I can handle–or more than we can handle together. I try to rely on my own strength, but I get tired. So I trust You to do what I can't. Energize me. Renew my strength. Give me the endurance to survive and thrive, no matter what tests of strength I encounter. Thank You for working in me to give me a second wind, for renewing my strength, and for showing me how Your grace is enough for any situation life throws my way.

AMEN.

EMBRACE REAL LOVE

Love must be free of hypocrisy.
Detest what is evil; cling to what is good.

ROMANS 12:9 NASB

Real love is unmistakable. If you've been burned by relationships in the past, you may have a cynical view of love. If you've watched people say one thing and do another, you may have no stomach for hypocrisy. Real love cuts through cynicism and contains no trace of hypocrisy. Real love isn't tainted by jealousy, rivalry, pettiness, or mood swings. Real love wants only what's best for a person. Real love involves sacrifice. Real love comes from God, and it changes lives forever. God loves us so much that He sent Jesus to take the punishment we deserve for the things we've done wrong. God sacrificed His only Son for us so that we can have eternal life. If we accept God's gift, His love will fill us. More than that, it will unlock something inside us that makes it possible for us to show real love to others. After God changes our lives forever, we can help change others.

God, thank You for making me feel loved. Thank You for showing me the kind of love I've never experienced before. Open my heart to Your love. Help me get rid of my cynicism, doubt, and feelings of unworthiness so that I can embrace it. I am awed and humbled by the sacrifice at the heart of Your love. Thank You for sending Your Son so that I can live forever with You. Let Your love work in me. Make me aware of any hypocrisy in my life and help me get rid of it before it becomes an obstacle to others.

TEACH ME TO DETEST WHAT IS EVIL AND CLING TO WHAT IS GOOD. AMEN.

JESUS CAN EMPATHIZE

For we do not have a high priest
who is unable to empathize with our weaknesses,
but we have one who has been tempted in every way,
just as we are—yet He did not sin.
Let us then approach God's throne of grace with confidence,
so that we may receive mercy and
find grace to help us in our time of need.

HEBREWS 4:15-16 NIV

No one can know what you're going through unless he's experienced what you have—the good, the bad, and the ugly. On the other hand, if someone has gone through what you're going through, he can guide you through it and offer you hope. That's the point this passage drives home. Jesus lived among us as one of us. He experienced pain, rejection, joy, sadness, disappointment, and temptation. He knows what you're going through, whatever it is. Yet Jesus never once let His experiences distract Him from doing God's will. He lived a perfect life. That made it possible for Him to bridge the gap that sin created between us and God. So Jesus not only guides us, but He also makes it possible for us to have a relationship with God.

God, thank You for sending Your Son to live among us. You sacrificed something unimaginable so that Jesus could become our perfect savior, high priest, and guide. Because of Jesus, I can approach You in prayer and pour out my heart to You without fear of rejection, knowing You will listen to me, care for me, and provide for me. Thank You that Jesus understands our pain, rejection, temptation, disappointment, and anything else we experience. Thank You that I can bring all my concerns and anxieties to You any time and find the help I need.

AMEN.

PRACTICE SPIRITUAL SELF-CARE

Or do you not know that your body is a temple of the Holy Spirit within you, whom you have from God, and that you are not your own? For you have been bought for a price: therefore glorify God in your body.

I CORINTHIANS 6:19-20 NASB

What do Mount Vernon, Monticello, and the Hermitage have in common? All are houses that were built over one hundred years ago. So why were these three houses deemed worthy of preservation? They were owned by Presidents George Washington, Thomas Jefferson, and Andrew Jackson, respectively. Their value is due to their occupants. The same principle lies at the heart of this passage from I Corinthians. Your body has tremendous value because it was created by God. But that's not the only reason it's worthy of extensive care and preservation. You see, when you follow Jesus, God takes up residence inside you. He guides and comforts you from within. That's why God's Word places such a high priority on spiritual self-care. You're not just taking care of your body; you're taking care of God's temple.

God, thank You for staying close to me always. Thank You for guiding me from within. Make Yourself at home in my heart. Change what needs to be changed so I become more like Jesus. Let me never lose sight of the high value You've placed on me. Let me see myself as You see me. Help me understand what it means that my body is a temple. Give me the discipline to maintain my physical, mental, emotional, and spiritual health.

LET MY BODY ALWAYS BE A PLACE WHERE YOU FEEL WELCOME.

AMEN.

FIND REAL CONTENTMENT

Not that I speak in regard to need,
for I have learned in whatever state I am, to be content.

PHILIPPIANS 4:11 NKJV

There are a lot of things a person could say to spark envy in someone else. "I have front-row tickets." "I'll be spending the weekend at my beach house." "I just got a full ride to medical school." But these words of Paul in Philippians are hard to beat. *No matter what state I'm in, I've learned to be content*. Paul could be content anywhere, with anything. His joy and satisfaction didn't depend on his circumstances. He could find reason to celebrate God's goodness to him 24-7. The fact that Paul was in prison when he wrote these words drives his point home. Contentment isn't a feeling you get when you have everything you want; it's a choice you make every day. If you *choose* to be content, you learn to see God's blessings all around. You develop a spirit of gratitude and joy. And you become a catalyst for other people's joy as well.

God, thank You for making it possible for me to be content, regardless of my circumstances. Thank You for the blessings that I can see. Open my eyes to the blessings I can't see. Give me a sense of the full scope of Your compassion and care for me. Help me lay the foundation for a spirit of contentment in my life. Thank You for not always giving me what I want. Let me learn from those experiences so that I can keep my heart from chasing things You know I don't need and shouldn't have. Keep me from coveting what others possess. And give me the clearness of mind to choose contentment every morning.

AMEN.

PLANT WISELY

Don't be deceived: God is not mocked. For whatever a person sows he will also reap.

GALATIANS 6:7 CSB

When God gave us His Word, He said (in effect), "If you want to know My will, if you want to find your purpose in life, if you want to experience true fulfillment, if you want to make a difference in the world, if you want to get a glimpse of eternity—dive in. In these pages, you'll find truth. You'll find the wisdom you need to make the best possible choices in any situation. You'll find comfort when you're hurting. You'll find light when things get dark. The more time and effort you put in to learning what My Word says, the bigger the impact it will have on your life. On the other hand, if you ignore My Word, if you choose to get your wisdom from other sources, your life will reflect those choices too. For better or worse, what you plant, you will harvest."

God, thank You for giving me the seeds to plant wisely in my life. Everything I need for an amazing harvest is in the pages of the Bible. Your Word can help me recognize my potential. Your Word can comfort me when I struggle. Your Word can motivate me when I'm down. Your Word can coax me out of my comfort zone. Your Word can inspire me to use the gifts I've been given. Your Word can show me what my priorities should be. Your Word can give me lessons for living that can be found nowhere else. Help me sow the seeds of your Word throughout my life. Nurture them and make them grow.

LET ME DISCOVER WHAT A RICH HARVEST LOOKS LIKE.

AMEN.

THE PURSUIT OF WEALTH

"No one can serve two masters, for either he will hate the one and love the other, or he will be devoted to the one and despise the other. You cannot serve God and money."

MATTHEW 6:24 ESV

Like a human master, the pursuit of money can take control of a person's life. This pursuit demands time and effort. It promises ultimate pleasure and fulfillment if people will dedicate themselves to it. But money rarely delivers. Unfortunately, most people don't discover the hollowness of its promises until it's too late. They pursue wealth aggressively and jettison things from their life that might slow their pursuit. They sacrifice family, friendships, and even their health chasing the almighty dollar. And when they get it, they discover that either it's never enough or money truly can't buy happiness. God, on the other hand, is a generous, merciful, and trustworthy Master. If you serve Him, you will be rewarded—in this life and for eternity. You will experience His goodness in big ways and small. You will discover that His promises can be trusted. You will find contentment and joy. And you will realize that serving God was the best choice you ever made.

God, thank You for being generous. I experience Your blessings every day. Help me to remain content no matter how much or how little I have. Thank You for being merciful. You forgive me when I fail. Thank You for being trustworthy. I can put my faith in Your promises. The pursuit of money may try to tempt me and take my focus off serving You, but I know what kind of master it is. I want to serve You. Please help me to use whatever money and possessions

YOU HAVE GIVEN ME
TO HELP OTHERS AND
BRING GLORY TO YOU.
AMEN.

WHEN YOU ARE WEAK, GOD IS STRONG

But He said to me, "My grace is sufficient for you, for My power is perfected in weakness." Therefore, I will most gladly boast all the more about my weaknesses, so that Christ's power may reside in me.

II CORINTHIANS 12:9 CSB

Paul wrote these words when he was discouraged. For years, he'd been bothered by what he called "a thorn in the flesh"—some kind of affliction that he believed kept him from reaching his full potential as a Christian minister. Three times he begged God to take away the affliction. And three times God said no. Paul saw only two options for his future: either God would take away his affliction so that Paul could thrive in his ministry or God would ignore his affliction and allow Paul's ministry to suffer. God had in mind a third option: Paul's affliction would cause him to lean on God for help instead of relying on his own strength. And his ministry would thrive because of it. It didn't take long for Paul to see the wisdom of God's plan. He discovered that God's strength is much more obvious when we are weak.

God, thank You for helping me see the big picture when it comes to personal afflictions. Thank You for helping me see possibilities instead of challenges. Thank You for the people who have inspired me by thriving while dealing with their own afflictions. Help me learn from their examples. Forgive me when I doubt You or grow frustrated. Help me discover the same thing about my own physical, mental, emotional, or spiritual weaknesses that Paul discovered about his thorn in the flesh. Give me the endurance to thrive despite my personal challenges. Remind me to lean on You when things get tough.

NEVER LET ME LOSE SIGHT OF YOUR STRENGTH.

AMEN.

ENDURE TRIALS

"These things I have spoken to you so that in Me you may have peace. In the world you have tribulation, but take courage; I have overcome the world."

JOHN 16:33 NASB

Did you know that tigers have white markings that look like "false eyes" on the back of their ears to keep predators from attacking them from behind? When that fact was posted in an online forum, someone pointed out that it made him feel less scared of the tiger and more scared of whatever the tiger considered a predator. Jesus made a similar point two thousand years ago. In this verse from John, He said to His followers, "There are a lot of things that seem scary in this world. You're going to face situations that threaten your well-being and rob you of your hope. Trials and tribulations will prey on your courage and mess with your sense of peace. But don't be afraid because I am more powerful than anything you will ever face." The problems and trials that loom so large in our daily lives are dwarfed by Jesus's power.

God, thank You for this promise in Your Word. Thank You for reminding me of Jesus's strength. Daily trials and tribulations have a way of altering my perspective. The more intense they become, the more unconquerable they seem. But I know that's an illusion. Help me remember Jesus's words when my struggles start to seem overwhelming. Give me the perspective to recognize how small they are compared to His power. Give me the courage to face my struggles knowing that their hold over me has already been broken. Help me approach them with the confidence of someone who knows he has all the backup he needs.

AMEN.

LET THE BIBLE DO ITS WORK

For the word of God is alive and active.
Sharper than any double-edged sword, it penetrates
even to dividing soul and spirit, joints and marrow;
it judges the thoughts and attitudes of the heart.

HEBREWS 4:12 NIV

The Bible is no ordinary book, as this verse makes clear. It's doubtful that any readers ever described *The Great Gatsby* as "alive and active." Or *Moby Dick* as penetrating to the core of their being. Yet the Bible checks both of those boxes. The sword imagery may seem a little confusing, and violent, to modern readers—unless you think of the double-edged blade as a scalpel. In the right hands, a scalpel can cut away unhealthy parts of a person and bring healing. That's what the Bible does. When you read it, certain passages seem to leap off the page. That's what it means to be "alive and active." They seem as though they were written specifically to you. They calm your anxiety. They answer your questions. They reveal promises of God that change your entire outlook. They help you understand what's really troubling you—what's going on deep inside your soul. They point to what needs to be cut out and how to heal.

God, thank You for the amazing power of Your Word. I want to harness that power in my life. But it's hard to know where to start or what to look for when I open its pages. Help me overcome my intimidation. Give me the patience and wisdom to find a reading strategy that works for me. Clear my mind of distractions so that passages jump off the page at me. Help me find the resources and mentors I need to help me understand what the Bible says and apply it to my life.

AMEN.

REST FOR THE WEARY

"Come to Me, all you who labor and are heavy laden, and I will give you rest."

MATTHEW 11:28 NKJV

Look closely at Jesus's words in this passage and you'll find two important clues in the search for contentment and fulfillment. Notice who Jesus's promise of rest is given to: "All you who labor." Jesus is a staunch ally of hard workers—and for good reason. Work and rest are key components of life on earth. God intends them to be a constant cycle, with one never dominating the other. Work gives us purpose and a sense of accomplishment that contribute mightily to our overall well-being. One of the first things God did after creating man was to assign him work. Adam was given the responsibility of tending the garden of Eden. Work is part of the human identity—and part of what it means to be created in God's image. The same goes for rest. God rested after working six days to create the world. It's a precedent He wants us to follow. Just as we are meant to work, we are meant to rest—physically, mentally, emotionally, and spiritually.

God, thank You for caring about my sense of contentment and fulfillment. Thank You for entrusting me with work that will help me achieve those things. Give me the perspective to approach work as You intend. Never let me lose sight of its importance and necessity. Help me see it for the blessing it is. Remind me that it isn't a necessary evil or a drudgery that I have to endure until retirement. Help me understand the importance and necessity of rest too. Give me the wisdom to know when I need to recharge and refresh.

HELP ME FIND THE RIGHT BALANCE BETWEEN WORK AND REST.

AMEN.

CELEBRATE CREATIVITY

So God created human beings, making them to be like Himself. He created them male and female.

GENESIS 1:27 GNT

The first five words of the Bible are "In the beginning God created." He is the original Creator. He started with the heavens and the earth and finished with human beings. And when He got to His final creative work, He added a signature move for the ages. He created man and woman in His own image. He instilled in us aspects of Himself—including the ability to create. God celebrates the creative process. He wants us to exercise our creative ability. The greatest poets, painters, and writers have found their inspiration in the natural world. That's no accident. God created a beautiful and mysterious world. He invites us to linger over it, celebrate it, notice its intricate details, and filter it through our own imaginations. He encourages us to explore what it means to be human, to exist in this universe. He equips us to create beauty and challenge each other's thinking. God revels in the creative process and wants us to as well.

God, thank You for Your awesome creative work. Thank You for the creativity that exists in me. You didn't put me in this world to be a passive spectator. You encourage me to take it all in. To appreciate the stunning details. To question its mysteries. To draw inspiration from it. Open my eyes to different sources of beauty and wonder in the world, things I may not have noticed or fully appreciated before. Help me find new and exciting ways to channel my creativity. Give me a deeper appreciation for Your creative work. Help me understand You better so that I can build a relationship with You.

AMEN

GOD WILL SUPPLY YOUR NEEDS

And this same God who takes care of me will supply all your needs from His glorious riches, which have been given to us in Christ Jesus.

PHILIPPIANS 4:19 NLT

I've got a guy." When you need something done, those four words, spoken by a trustworthy friend or acquaintance, can make all the difference in the world. Need to recover data from a hard drive? *I've got a guy.* Need a backed-up drain unclogged? *I've got a guy.* Need to diagnose a problem with your car's alignment? *I've got a guy.* Those four words can take the edge off almost any minor crisis. They imply that the "guy" in question has been tested before and has proven himself trustworthy. For Paul, the man who wrote Philippians, God is "the guy"—in a much larger sense, of course. When people fret about where to turn to for hope when life turns dark or how to overcome a seemingly insurmountable problem, this message of Paul offers a definitive answer: "I've got a guy."

God, thank You for being "the guy." Thank You for always being available. You see everything, so You know the problems and crises I face even before I do. You created me, so You understand my needs even better than I do. You also know my wants. Help me recognize the difference between the two. Let me never lose sight of Your promise to supply all my needs, especially when things get tense. You have been tested countless times and have always proven Yourself to be trustworthy. I know that I can depend on You, even when I go through tough times. Everything I need, You will supply.

SO HELP ME LEARN TO BE CONTENT WITH WHAT YOU GIVE. AMEN.

GIVE CHEERFULLY

Each one must give as he has decided in his heart, not reluctantly or under compulsion, for God loves a cheerful giver.

II CORINTHIANS 9:7 ESV

Everything that's good and useful in your life comes from God. And, chances are, if you do a mental inventory of the good and useful things in your life, you'll be surprised by how generous God is. Your inventory would include not just your income and material possessions but also your health, skills, abilities, family, friends, and opportunities. The decision of the heart that Paul refers to in this verse is whether you want to be the owner of those things or the steward of them. An owner hoards. He looks at God's blessings in his life and says, "These are all for me." A steward looks at those same blessings and asks, "How can I make the best possible use of them?" And the answer is usually to redirect those blessings to where they can have maximum impact. That's where the cheerfulness and excitement of giving comes from—knowing that you're working with God to make a difference in the world, one generous act at a time.

God, thank You for being such an incredible giver. I know that everything good in my life comes from You. I also know that for every one thing I can think of that You've given me, there are one hundred more that I can't think of. Help me understand the difference between being an owner of Your blessings and being a steward of them. Give me a sense of how I can use them generously to help others. Thank You for the opportunity to work with You to make the world a better place.

LET ME NEVER LOSE SIGHT OF WHAT A PRIVILEGE IT IS. AMEN.

EMBRACE HUMILITY

When arrogance comes, disgrace follows,
but with humility comes wisdom.

PROVERBS 11:2 CSB

Solomon, the writer of most of Proverbs, understood God as well as a human being can. And in this verse, he lets his readers in on a little secret: God gives wisdom to His people who are humble. If you look at the major characters in the Bible—the ones who God spoke to and who played key roles in His miracles—the one thing they have in common is humility. They didn't act prideful about the amazing things God did in their lives. So when those amazing things happened, God was the one who got all the credit. And that's the way it should be. Humble people are awed by God's grace. They're quick to give Him glory for the good things that happen in their lives. That's why they share a special bond with Him. If you're unsure about how to approach God, start with a humble attitude. You'll be amazed by how He responds.

God, Your Word guides us in how You want us to live. Micah 6:8 says that You want us to "act justly, to love faithfulness, and to walk humbly" with You (CSB). That is what I want to do: walk humbly with You. I come to You now with a humble spirit. Thank You for giving me such specific instructions for how to connect with You. I admit that the line between confidence and arrogance is sometimes hard to see. Help me figure out how to develop an attitude that You consider good. Please give me wisdom so I can better know what humility looks like in my life so that I can walk humbly with You.

AMEN.

HONOR YOUR MARRIAGE

Marriage is to be held in honor by all,
and the marriage bed is to be undefiled;
for God will judge the sexually immoral and adulterers.

HEBREWS 13:4 NASB

Genesis 1–2 tells the story of the six days of creation, in which God brought the world as we know it into existence. His final act, as the sixth day was drawing to a close, was to create marriage. "A man shall leave his father and his mother, and be joined to his wife; and they shall become one flesh" (Genesis 2:24 NASB). This verse in Hebrews reminds us to honor God's sacred creation. If you're not married, you can support those who are. If you're married, honor marriage by celebrating your wife and the life you've built together. Honor it by enjoying an exclusive sexual relationship with your wife, learning how to please one another for a lifetime. Honor it by not taking it for granted, by putting in the necessary work to improve your relationship. Honor it by maintaining a spirit of gratitude for it.

God, thank You for Your amazing gift of marriage. Thank You for allowing two people to experience such a close, intimate relationship as they walk through the ups and downs of life together and learn more about what it means to follow You together. Thank You for the relationship math that makes it possible for two to become one. Let me never take marriage for granted or treat it as anything but an amazing gift. Thank You for giving us Your Word that shows us how special marriage is and how You designed it. Please bless the marriages of the people in my life. Protect them from anything that would threaten to break their sacred bond.

AMEN.

BE TRANSFORMED, NOT CONFORMED

Do not conform to the pattern of this world, but be transformed by the renewing of your mind. Then you will be able to test and approve what God's will is— His good, pleasing and perfect will.

ROMANS 12:2 NIV

Aim high. That's the message of this verse. Conformity may be the path of least resistance, but it doesn't lead anywhere. What good is it to be like everyone else when everyone else is settling for less than their best? The only way to reach your full potential is to let God transform you into the person He created you to be. Only He knows what you're truly capable of. Only He knows the path He's laid out for you as a transformed person. In many cases, being transformed means going against the pattern other people follow. The transformation begins by reading God's Word, absorbing its truths, and letting them guide the way you live. That's what makes it possible to do things like love your enemies, turn the other cheek, and embrace humility. That's what makes it possible to recognize God's will.

God, thank You for giving me an alternative to conformity. Thank You for seeing in me the potential to be transformed. I understand that transformation doesn't happen quickly or easily. I understand that the appeal of conforming to the culture around me is hard to resist. Give me the endurance to continue transforming for the rest of my life. Open my eyes to the wisdom in Your Word. Show me how to apply its truths to my daily life. Give me the courage to swim against the tide when I need to. Let me never lose sight of the person I'm striving to be.

HELP ME REACH
MY POTENTIAL IN YOUR EYES.
AMEN.

STAY NEAR TO GOD

The Lord is near to all who call upon Him,
to all who call upon Him in truth.

PSALM 145:18 NKJV

These words would make a great billboard ad for prayer. That's how we call upon the Lord: through prayer—heartfelt, continuous, one-on-one conversations with Him. The nearness this verse talks about doesn't come from occasional, desperate shouts for help—"911 prayers," where we expect God to rescue us from our immediate problem and then leave, like a first responder. It comes from frequent conversations in which we listen as much as we speak. That's how a friendship forms, and that's how a sense of nearness develops. Calling upon God "in truth" means understanding who He is. We can't ask Him to go against His nature and, say, reward greed or take revenge or honor misplaced priorities. That's not how closeness develops. The better we know Him, through reading His Word and communicating with Him, the more effective our prayers will be—and the closer we will get to Him.

God, thank You for being near to me. Thank You for encouraging me to pray. Help me wrap my head around the fact that the Creator of the universe wants to have one-on-one conversations with me. Have patience with me as I learn to balance talking and listening. Help me get closer to You by reading Your Word. Show me what You're like so that I can "call upon [You] in truth." Help me understand what You do and don't like. Please stay near me. Give me strength when I struggle. Give me courage when I'm scared. Give me encouragement when I'm down. Give me hope when things seem hopeless. Remind me that I'm never alone, no matter how lonely I feel.

AMEN.

DEFUSE ARGUMENTS

But keep away from foolish and ignorant arguments;
you know that they end up in quarrels.
As the Lord's servant, you must not quarrel.
You must be kind toward all, a good and patient teacher,
who is gentle as you correct your opponents,
for it may be that God will give them
the opportunity to repent and come to know the truth.
And then they will come to their senses
and escape from the trap of the Devil,
who had caught them and made them obey his will.

II TIMOTHY 2:23–26 GNT

God's wisdom is on full display in this passage. On the one hand, He understands the passions involved when people defend their beliefs. On the other hand, He knows how those passions can go awry in the heat of battle. So He advises a brilliant debate strategy built on kindness, goodness, and patience. Kindness and goodness not only lower the temperature of a debate, but they also lower people's defenses, making them more likely to listen. In return, our patience lets them know that they're being heard. Arguments don't have to be "won" on the spot. God can plant seeds of His truth in people's hearts that take root and blossom long after a debate ends.

God, thank You for promoting peace. Thank You for reminding me that foolish arguments accomplish nothing. Give me the wisdom to recognize a foolish argument when it begins. Give me the words to de-escalate the situation. Give me the confidence to walk away from it. Help me tap into my kindness, goodness, and patience when I encounter someone who opposes me. Remind me that I don't have to win. Remind me that You can plant a seed in that person's life that will grow long after the debate ends

AMEN.

USE YOUR GOD-GIVEN GIFT

God has given each of you a gift
from His great variety of spiritual gifts.
Use them well to serve one another.

I PETER 4:10 NLT

God gives everyone who follows Jesus a spiritual gift—an ability he can use to help others. Discovering and using your spiritual gift is an important step in growing in the Christian faith. The "great variety of spiritual gifts" mentioned in this verse can be found in passages such as Romans 12 and I Corinthians 12–13. To discover your gift, start by reading through these passages to see if any of the gifts resonate with you. Think about what you enjoy doing or what comes naturally to you. Do any of the gifts align with those things? Think about the qualities other people see in you. You may find clues there. Once you have an idea of your God-given gift, look for ways to put it to use. Most churches offer a variety of ministries and a variety of ways to use spiritual gifts. Find a church that feels right to you and get started!

God, thank You for giving me a special ability to make a difference in this world. Give me guidance and direction as I try to figure out what my gift is and how I can put it to use. Help me look objectively at myself to see if any of my skills and abilities line up with the spiritual gifts listed in the Bible. Give me patience and motivation through the trial and error of figuring out my spiritual gift. Help me find a church connection where I can learn more. Surround me with people who are also trying to use their spiritual gifts.

HELP ME RECOGNIZE THE BEST WAYS TO USE THE ABILITIES YOU'VE GIVEN ME.

AMEN.

FAITHFULLY ENDURE

Resist him, firm in your faith,
knowing that the same kinds of suffering are being
experienced by your brotherhood throughout the world.
And after you have suffered a little while,
the God of all grace, who has called you
to his eternal glory in Christ, will himself restore,
confirm, strengthen, and establish you.

I PETER 5:9–10 ESV

God's enemy, the devil, uses his limited power to make God's people suffer. His strategy is to drive a wedge between us and God by convincing us that God is responsible for our suffering. This verse reveals a three-part counterstrategy that tips our spiritual battle in our favor. First, stand firm. Weather the initial blast. Hold tight to your faith in Jesus. Pray for the strength to endure suffering. Second, draw strength from numbers. Share your struggles with others. Encourage and pray for one another. Third, remind yourself that the end of your struggle is in sight. "A little while" may not seem like a little while when you're suffering—but your suffering *will* end. And God will reward your faithful endurance. Let the knowledge fill you with confidence and hope.

God, thank You for Your reassurance in this passage. I know that suffering is part of living this life on earth. Please help me to recognize that You are not the One responsible for suffering but that You are the One whom I can turn to in the midst of suffering. Please give me the endurance to stand firm in my faith even when I struggle with difficulties in this life. Give me the courage and confidence to endure suffering when it comes. Help me trust in Your promise that it will be temporary.

THANK YOU FOR THE HOPE AND THE JOY I HAVE IN TRUSTING YOU. AMEN.

TAKE RESPONSIBILITY

The one who conceals his sins will not prosper,
but whoever confesses and renounces them will find mercy.

PROVERBS 28:13 CSB

The 1986 film *The Mission* features a memorable scene in which a guilt-ridden eighteenth-century slave trader in South America struggles to climb a mountain. He lugs a huge bundle tied to his back as a penance for his evil ways. He barely makes it to the top, where he's surrounded by the Guarani people, whose tribe he had terrorized. One tribesman holds a knife to his throat, but then cuts the bundle free, dropping it into a river far below Like that scene, this verse from Proverbs offers a powerful reminder to anyone who carries a burden of guilt: you don't have to. Forgiveness and mercy are just a confession away. The urge to hide the things we do wrong and internalize our guilt is strong. But we can't be forgiven for things we won't admit. And we *can* be forgiven for *anything* for which we're truly sorry—if we have the courage to confess and renounce it.

God, thank You for Your mercy. I understand that I can do nothing to earn Your forgiveness. You offer it purely out of love for me. Remind me of Your mercy when I try to carry my guilt alone. Help me understand that trying to hide something I've done wrong accomplishes nothing. It only makes matters worse. Give me the courage to admit what I've done wrong–to myself and, more importantly, to You. Help me understand that confessing it is the first step in being free from it. Remind me that Your forgiveness and mercy last forever.

YOU WILL NEVER REMEMBER
MY WRONGDOING AGAIN.
AMEN.

START WITH YOURSELF

"Why do you look at the speck that is in your brother's eye, but do not notice the log that is in your own eye? Or how can you say to your brother, 'Let me take the speck out of your eye,' and look, the log is in your own eye? You hypocrite, first take the log out of your own eye, and then you will see clearly to take the speck out of your brother's eye!"

MATTHEW 7:3-5 NASB

Jesus offers helpful advice to people who have an urge to judge others or tell them what they're doing wrong. He says look at yourself first. Think of the actions and attitudes you object to in other people and see if you can find any traces of them in yourself. If you're unable to be objective where you're concerned, ask people you trust to weigh in. This self-analysis that Jesus prescribes accomplishes two things. First, it helps you identify problem areas you may be unaware of. Second, it gives you empathy for others. If you realize that you struggle with a similar problem, you're more likely to be understanding of other strugglers. And empathy is a great foundation for a friendship.

God, thank You for giving me this helpful reminder to not point fingers at others. Please give me the humility to look first at myself and deal with the things I need to work on. Let the truth in Your Word guide me in my interactions with people. Remind me of them when I'm tempted to judge or confront. Guide me in doing a self-examination to find areas in need of fixing in my own life. Help me live authentically, without hypocrisy.

I WANT TO EMPATHIZE WITH PEOPLE AND LOVE THEM, NOT CRITICIZE AND JUDGE THEM. AMEN.

SET YOUR PRIORITIES

"But seek first His kingdom and His righteousness, and all these things will be given to you as well."

MATTHEW 6:33 NIV

Here's the secret to unlocking life's full potential: placing our priorities in the correct order. Our default program is to put ourselves first—to set our preferred agenda, to focus on our own needs, to satisfy our personal desires. The problem is, when we turn our focus inward, we lose sight of what God has planned for us. That's why He says, "Look to Me first. Focus on building a solid relationship with Me. Learn My Word. Follow My instructions. Stay in close contact through prayer. I'll take care of you—better than you can take care of yourself. The difference is, I'll add things that make your life truly fulfilling and satisfying. I'll open your eyes to people who need you and surround you with others who invest themselves in you. I'll show you strength you never knew you had, gifts you never dreamed you possessed, and opportunities you never would have had otherwise."

God, thank You for showing me how to experience life to the fullest. Thank You for showing me where to place my priorities. In the busyness of daily life, help me keep my priorities in order. Remind me why it's important to keep my focus outward, when I really want to focus on myself. Show me what happens when I trust in the promises of the Bible and make decisions based on its truths. Help me recognize the good things You bring into my life as a result. Give me a sense of the strength and gifts I possess.

SHOW ME HOW TAKE ADVANTAGE OF EVERY OPPORTUNITY YOU OFFER.

AMEN.

RESIST THE DEVIL

Therefore submit to God.
Resist the devil and he will flee from you.

JAMES 4:7 NKJV

The devil is the enemy of everyone who follows Jesus. The Bible describes him as a crafty foe who studies us carefully, looking for vulnerabilities he can exploit. He tried to do this with Jesus. Matthew 4:1–11 tells us how the devil prepared multiple temptations for Jesus. His goal was to prevent Jesus from saving humanity. Jesus didn't use supernatural forces to battle the devil. He used something much more powerful: He quoted God's Word. Three times the devil tried to lure Jesus away from His mission, and three times Jesus spoke words from the Bible. The devil realized he was overmatched and left. That's what submitting to God looks like: relying on His Word, His will, and His way because they are much better, much more powerful, and much more effective than ours. When we do that, all the enemy can do is flee.